To Phil & Ruth,
Most regards and I sincerely
hope you enjoy the book!
Cheers,

[signature] 12 Oct 96

For Gail, a true angel.

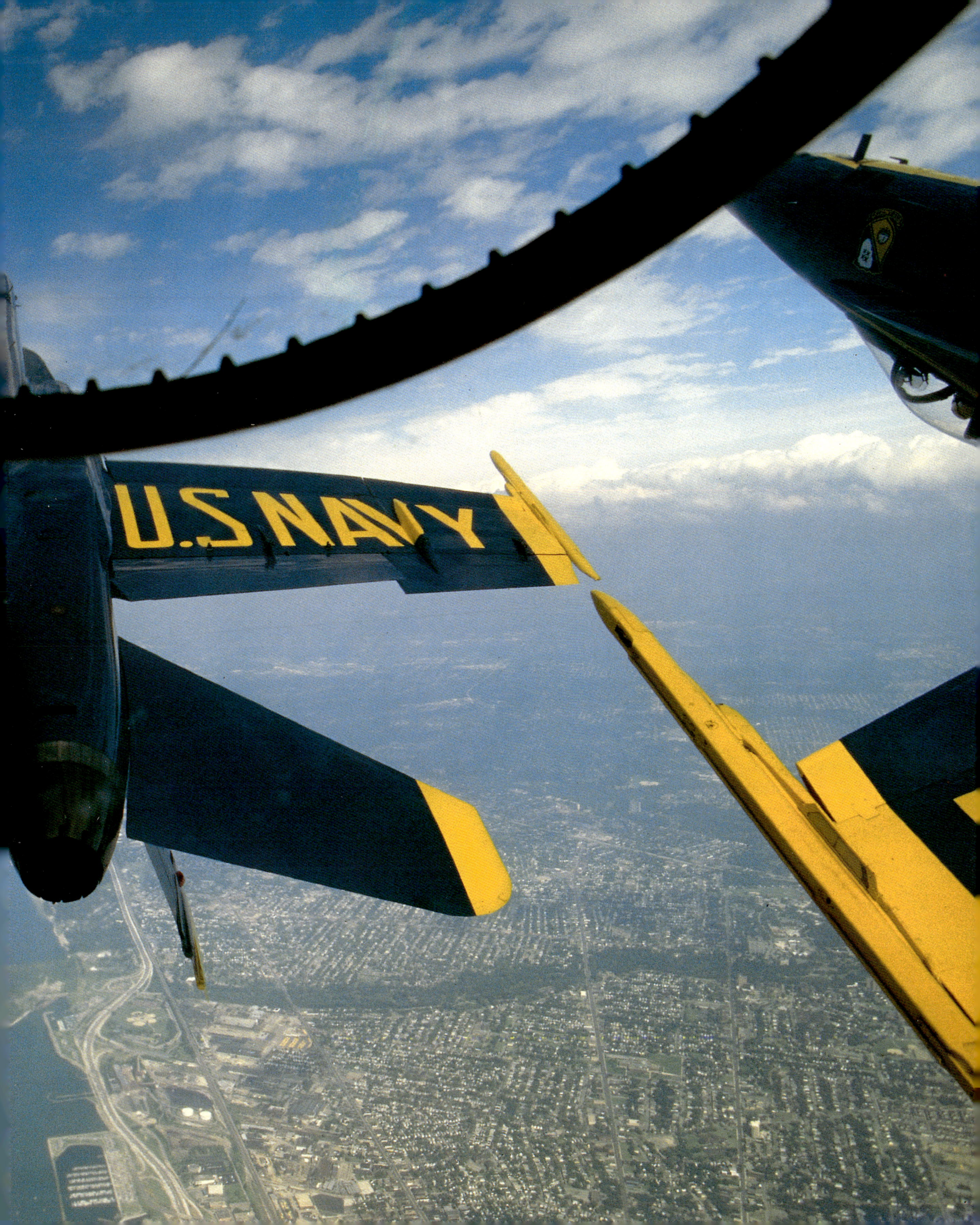
U.S NAVY

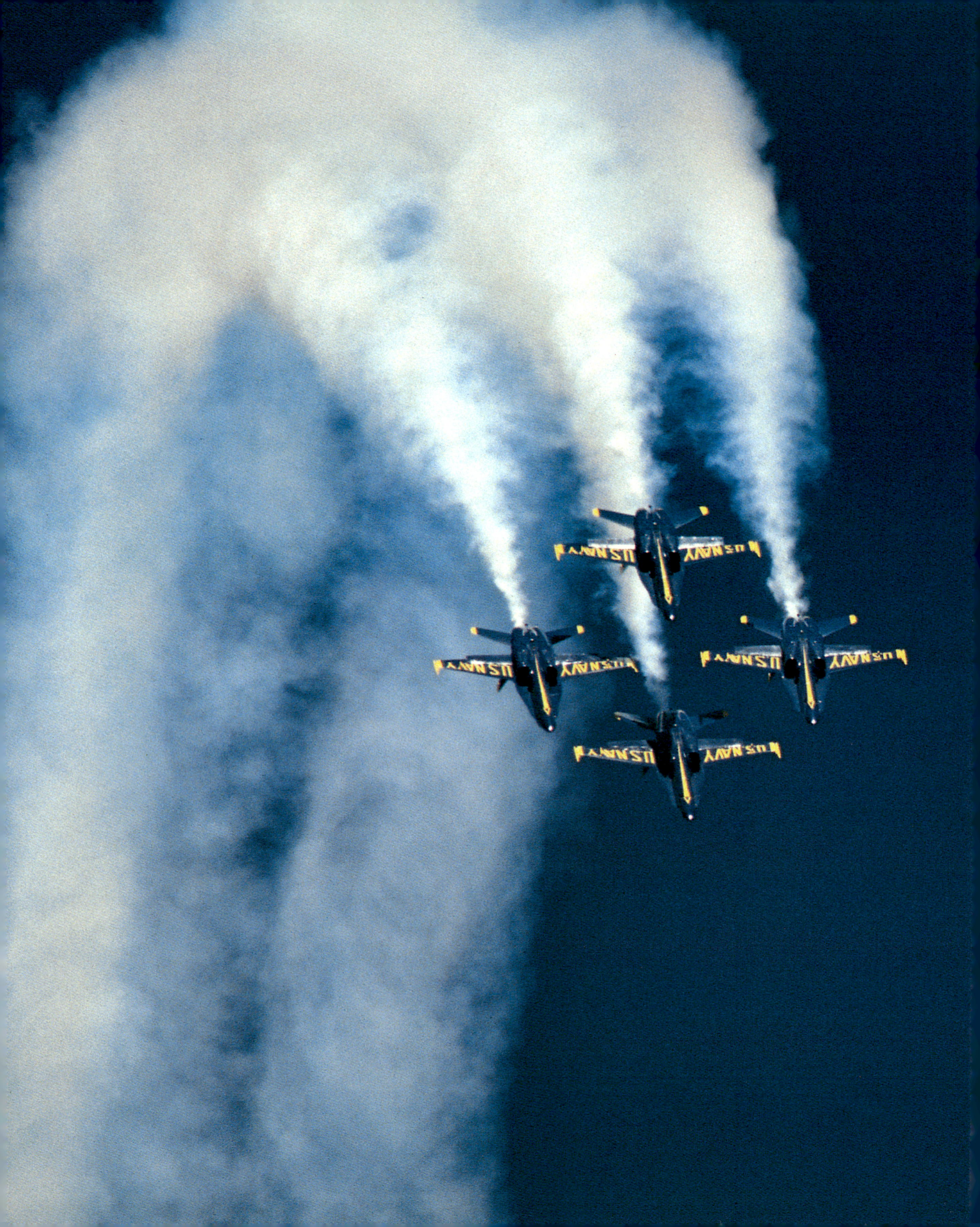
U.S. NAVY

Blue Angels
A Portrait of Gold

By Brian Shul

Mach 1, Inc. *Chico, California*

Blue Angels
A Portrait of Gold

Alpha
Bravo
Charlie
Delta
Echo
Foxtrot
Golf
Hotel
India
Juliet
Kilo
Lima
Mike
November
Oscar
Papa
Quebec
Romeo
Sierra
Tango
Uniform
Victor
Whiskey
Xray
Yankee
Zulu

Published by MACH 1, Inc.
PO Box 7360, Chico CA 95927

Text Copyright © 1995 Brian Shul

Photographs © 1995 by Brian Shul
with the exception of page 15 © 1995 Brian Silcox
and pages 1 and 152 © 1995 Glenn Miyoda

Publication Design/ Daniel Salcedo
Chief Editor/ David Salcedo

Printed in Singapore by Craft Print Pte. Ltd.
Chief Production Advisor/ Koh Cheng Hwee

No part of this publication may be reproduced or used in any form or by any means — graphic, electronic, or mechanical, including photocopying, recording, taping, or information storage and retrieval systems — without written permission of the publisher.

Library of Congress Catalog Card Number 95-78732

ISBN 0-929823-40-0

First printing, October 1995

INTRODUCTION 7

Acknowledgements

With deepest thanks and appreciation, the following people are recognized for their help in the completion of this book: Lieutenant John Kirby, Captain Ed "Otto" Pernotto, William Orr, Jack Levine, Melody Elizabeth Dickison, Glenn Miyoda, Brian Silcox, Professor K. Bowles, Donnie Duncan, Dave Scheuer, Butch Voris, the crew of the show center boat at Traverse City, the folks manning the Burke-Lakefront Tower, the United States Coast Guard Detachment at Pensacola, the helpful staff at the Pensacola Naval Air Museum, and the entire 1994 Blue Angels team.

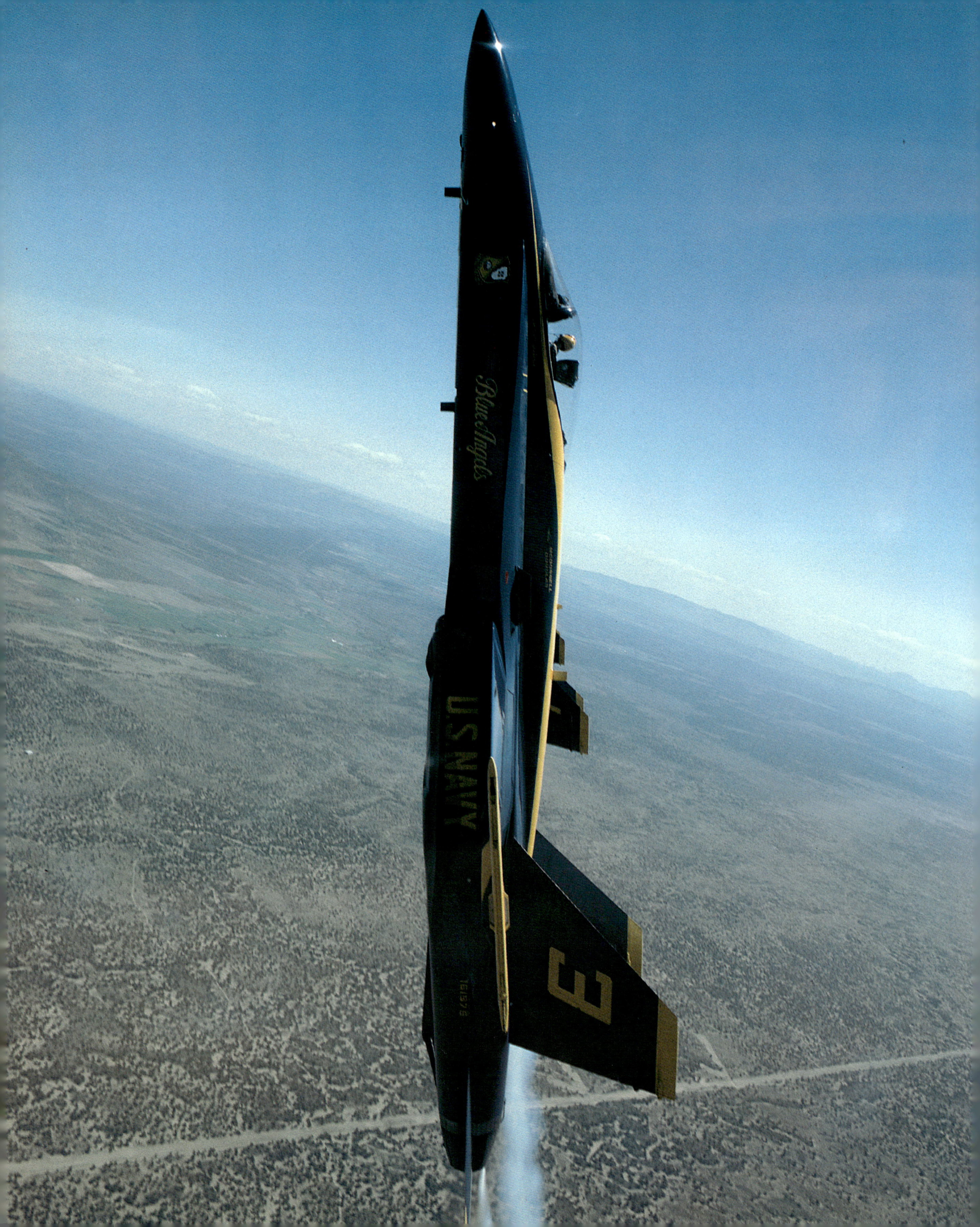
Blue Angels
U.S. NAVY
3

Preface

By Paul Farsai, Publisher

The United States Navy Blue Angels are America's oldest military flying demonstration team. Over the past 50 years, the Blue Angels have been loved and respected by millions throughout the world. There has long been a scarcity of written works about this renowned organization. Until now.

With the publication of *Blue Angels: A Portrait of Gold*, we are pleased to announce that Mach 1 has produced a singularly distinctive book about this world famous team. This was no small undertaking.

When we approached the Blue Angels with our request to produce this book, we realized we were seeking permission rarely granted by this prestigious team. The team, in response, enthusiastically invited us to spend an entire air show season with them in order to gain insight into the Blue Angel experience.

To take on this assignment, we sent the best of the best: award winning author, photographer, and former fighter pilot Brian Shul. In the course of that challenging year, he was given the unique opportunity to fly with the Blue Angels in all of their formations. With pen and camera, Brian Shul tells the Blue Angel story with a passion and an eye for detail that set his books apart. *Blue Angels: A Portrait of Gold* is an extraordinary record of the people who comprise a team steeped in a tradition of excellence.

We are honored that the United States Navy Blue Angels have entrusted Mach 1 with their story, and are proud to commemorate their golden anniversary.

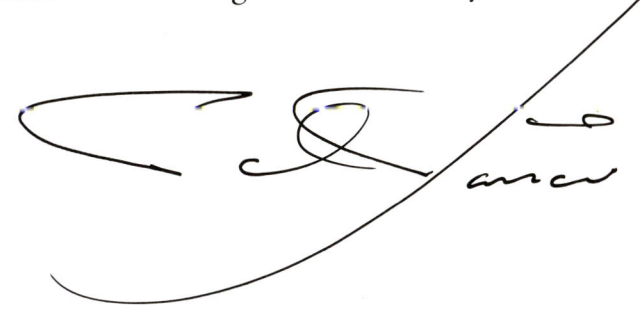

Paul Farsai, President, Mach 1, Incorporated

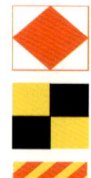

BLUE ANGELS *A Portrait of Gold*

CONTENTS

Blue Angels
A Portrait of Gold

	Preface	9
	Introduction	15
1	The Living Legend	23
2	The Rites of Spring	41
3	Home Base	57
4	Fat Albert	71
5	Feet Wet	87
6	Western Tour	101
7	The Seven Jet	121
8	Meeting of Giants	139
9	Autumn Gold	155
10	Silent Passage	169
	Epilogue	181
	Roll Call	186

NAVY *Blue Angels*

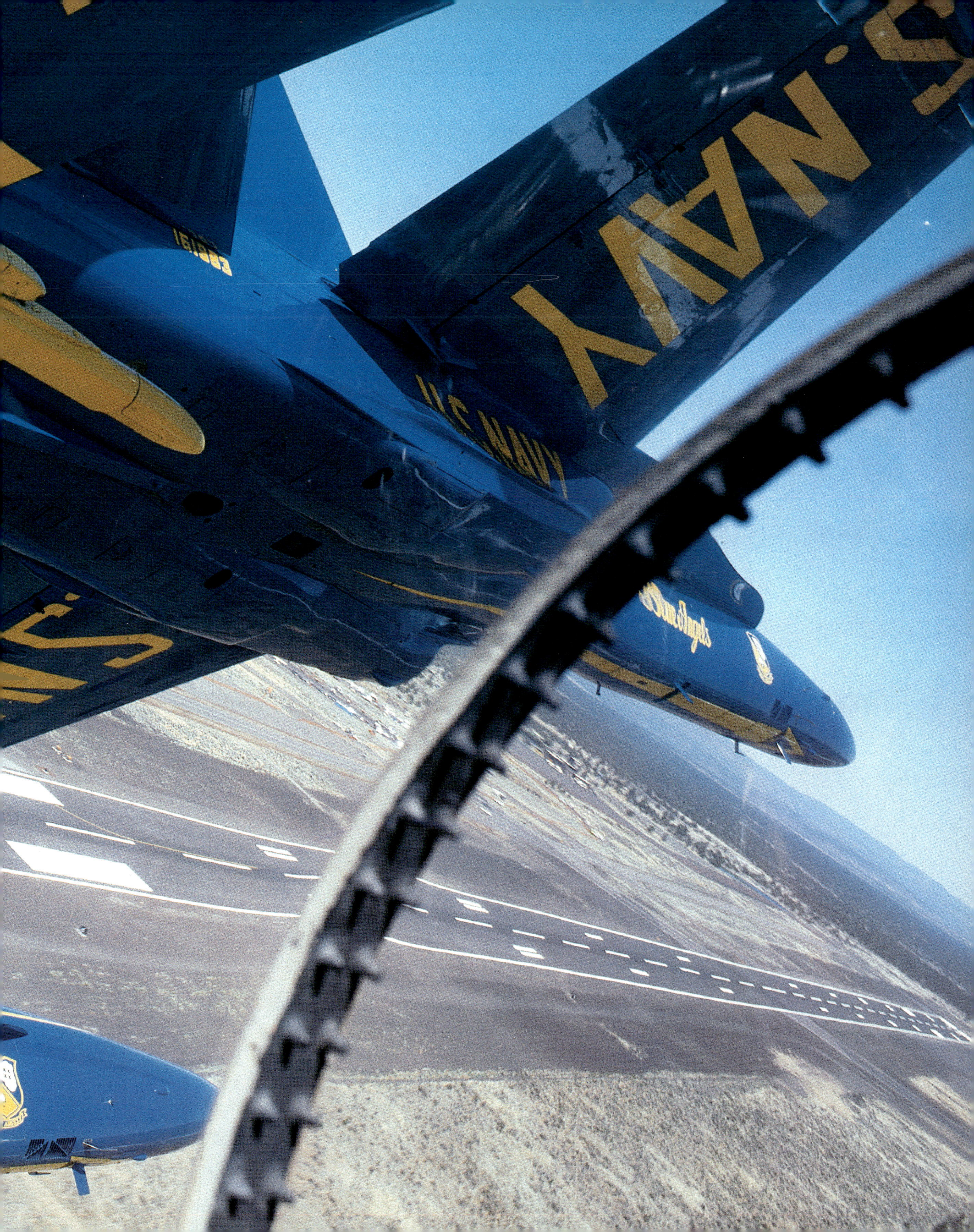

NAVY
U.S. NAVY
Blue Angels

14 BLUE ANGELS *A Portrait of Gold*

McDonnell Douglas F/A-18 Hornet, the Golden Anniversary mount of the Blue Angels. After 50 years, the aircraft are sleeker and much faster, yet much remains the same. It is still pull, turn, and roll.

INTRODUCTION

15

At the end of the Second World War, the Grumman F6F Hellcat was numerically the most important carrier-based fighter plane in use by the US Navy. With a victory ratio over Japanese planes of 19 to 1, the Hellcat ensured air superiority in the Pacific during the final years of the war. The close of hostilities brought with it a reduction in the size of the Armed Forces and a return to civilian life for many of the Navy's most experienced pilots. To enhance recruitment, the Navy saw a growing need for the public demonstration of American naval power through its air arm, and the Hellcat was called to serve as the first aircraft to be flown by the newly formed Navy Flight Exhibition Team.

Introduction
BY BUTCH VORIS

The time was early # 1946

We were young, all in our early to mid-twenties. World War II was behind us, and we looked to the future and to our respective naval careers. The Navy was faced with the challenge of resizing and restructuring its forces for its place in peacetime operations. No longer did the daily headlines recount the strength of the mighty naval attack carrier forces that had been so critical in assuring victory in the Pacific.

Maintaining the Navy's hard won position and keeping it highly visible would be a new and ongoing challenge for both civilian and military leaders. They recognized the importance of keeping the Navy's capabilities fresh in the minds of American citizens and their representatives in Washington.

Upon returning home after WW II, I had been instructing fighter tactics and was the Flight Officer in my organization. One morning, after being summoned by my boss, I was asked to give some thought as to how we could form a flight exhibition team, and to draw up some plans for such a project. This meeting resulted from a directive issued by the Secretary of the Navy and the Chief of Naval Operations. After expressing my thoughts and suggestions, I was instructed to work up a recommended flight routine, and to include the specific aircraft that would work for such a routine. Apparently, my recommendations were sufficient to gain final approval to go ahead with the project. I soon learned that I had been chosen and approved as Officer-in-Charge and Leader of a team, which initially would be named the Navy Flight Exhibition Team.

In retrospect, this was quite a bold move by the Navy Secretary and the Chief of Naval Operations. The allocation of personnel, aircraft, and funds to the training and operations of a flying exhibition team at a time of shrinking resources could well have been harshly criticized. However, they believed it was important to have such a team. This effort would demonstrate to the American people the quality of Navy personnel and machines that had so decisively defeated enemy air power at sea.

There would be those who might quickly dismiss it a stunt team, but it was far from that. We viewed it as a finely trained organization of wartime pilots, who, at low altitude, would demonstrate the maneuvers Navy fighter pilots used in air-to-air combat. The close formation flying would demonstrate the precision and skill needed to succeed in aerial combat.

I was given little, if any, guidance as to how to organize the team. There had been some Navy units flying air show routines before this, but nothing on this scale. I had no real model for comparison, so I approached the challenge with two opposing forces at work: be the best of all, while being safe, knowing that to fall short of either would be unacceptable.

My first concern was selecting the aircraft the team would use. I quickly narrowed the field to either the Corsair or the Hellcat, two great fighters. The Corsair, although sleeker in appearance, exhibited a vicious tendency to snap roll at slow speed in inverted flight, a characteristic unacceptable for close formation flying. The Hellcat got the nod. We took out the guns and armor plating and achieved a very decent power to weight ratio for those days.

I wanted to keep the demonstration low, tight, and close in to the crowd. There would be no slack for the pilots. We would get it up, get it on, and get it down in 17 minutes of pull, turn, and roll. All of this would be accomplished with heavy G forces on the planes for nearly the whole time. We had no idea of what to expect from the crowd, so I wanted to make the flight routine short. My goal was to keep it in front of the stands, thus never losing the attention of the spectators.

We flew in a three plane "V" formation. A particularly challenging maneuver for that first team in the "V" was to roll the planes in tight formation. Each plane would roll on their own axis, actually blind to each other during at least half of the roll. Later, the team would shift from the "V" to the diamond formation because the blind rolls carried too high of a risk. This was especially true considering the 12 foot diameter propellers, the thought of which could never be completely ignored. The diamond would later roll about the axis of the formation, altogether a much safer approach. In retrospect, however, I considered the close formation blind rolls a demonstration of the ultimate in areas of absolute trust and confidence in oneself and in each other.

I hand-picked that first team, and preferred that in addition to being superb pilots, they all be bachelors. This type of flying would put great physical and mental demands on the team, and I wanted their undivided attention. I chose men I knew I could count on in the clutch; men who had proven themselves in combat.

I knew that the unwritten purpose of it all was to influence the public, and to motivate young men to become naval aviators. Our basic motivation for excellence was to best our competition, the Army Air Corps. I figured if we could do this, it would surely impress the crowd. This meant pressing the envelope, while still controlling the risk. It is a delicate balance to achieve, the prospect of failure and death being ever present.

Our first show was in June of 1946 in Jacksonville, Florida. We were given no guidance, just simply told to go and do it. The only rules we had were those we imposed on ourselves. Officially, we were named the Naval Flight Exhibition Team, and I think a lot of Navy folks thought we would probably kill ourselves rather quickly. In keeping with Navy tradition, I adopted a very basic paint scheme for the planes. The design used a slightly lighter shade of blue than the fleet planes, and we dressed the planes with very conservative gold numerals. NAVY was displayed on the fuselage sides, and US NAVY on the lower surface of the wing. (I later found out that actual gold leaf had been used.) We wanted the aircraft to reflect the blue and gold unpretentious character of the Navy. That concept continues today; performance over flash.

Initially, logistics for travel were sort of pick-up, with little planned formality. At air show sites, we were generally taken care of by civilian air show authorities. We really had no idea how the public would receive us at that first show. I did know that there would be no in-between; we would either leave there highly successful or as a dismal failure.

INTRODUCTION 17

As Blue Angels pay tribute to one of their own during a retirement ceremony, a permanent diamond formation of McDonnell Douglas A-4F Skyhawks keeps a silent vigil over the Blue Angel wing of the Pensacola Naval Air Museum. The Skyhawk served the Blue Angels for thirteen years.

Fifty years have now passed since that first demonstration. To me, the memory of it has scarcely faded. We had trained hard and all went well in the show. Upon landing, we received a standing ovation from the thousands of spectators in the viewing stands. As we walked over to the fence to greet folks who had massed as close to our planes as they could, they began asking for our signatures on their programs. Thus, another air show tradition began. We had no idea it would ever become a permanent part of our routine.

The Navy was pleased, and, shortly thereafter, held a contest to name the team. We were told that the name Blue Lancers had been selected. This name didn't excite us much, but the son of a prominent Navy captain had submitted it, so we were in a bit of a bind.

We were preparing for a trip to Omaha for the World's Fair Aviation Meet, and then on to New York City. My #2 man was looking through the *New Yorker* for things to see while in the city when he came across an ad for the Blue Angel, a popular nightclub in those days. He stood up and said, "Boss, this is it!" And so it was. We all loved it. Yet we still had the problem of the Blue Lancer thing, so we used the media to give us a little help.

We had become pretty popular with the aviation press corps, and, while at Omaha, informed them of our dilemma. The day following our performance at the well-attended air show, the newspapers were filled with complimentary articles addressing us in bold headlines as THE BLUE ANGELS. Needless to say, the captain had a few questions for me when we returned from the trip. I feigned surprise at the headlines, and didn't fool him one bit as he threw me out of his office with half a smile. But the team had a name, one which became distinctively ours and in time, would be known and respected the world over.

We were on our way and found new challenges, as the team grew in popularity and increased its air show schedule. We had a small transport plane which carried four mechanics and a tool box – this was our support. One of the biggest difficulties was simply getting the planes to the different air shows around the country. Dodging weather, making numerous stops, and flying at those slow airspeeds in those days sometimes made flying the air show itself the least stressful thing we did.

I had the rare opportunity to become Team Leader for a second time during the Korean War. We were in jets then, and that made the routines a bit smoother. However, the increased speeds made it more difficult to get the formation turned around quickly. Thus, we used our solos to keep the show in front of the crowd, while the diamond repositioned.

It was during this time also that we pretty much established the Navy deep-stacked diamond formation. The stubby little Panther jet exhibited quite a severe downwash, and if #4 got up too shallow in the slot, he'd really move the Leader around. So we positioned the wingmen a bit deeper than normal on the Leader: it felt better, and we liked the way it made the formation look. It is still the team's trademark today and what makes ours the world's tightest formation.

No matter how good we got, it was, and still is, an inherently dangerous business flying jets so close while maneuvering. All of us understood this fact and accepted the risks involved. Along the way, there would be some bad days.

One morning, while leading the formation low across the water at Corpus Christi, I felt an increase in turbulence as we descended toward show center. My #4 man told everyone to move it out a bit because the air got very choppy. With no warning, the formation hit a pocket of severe turbulence, and my jet and #3 collided, causing him to lose three feet of his wing. My entire port stabilizer was sheared off, and the sudden, uncommanded pitch change in my aircraft caused my tail to shear off #4's nose. My jet then pitched over with such force that I could see only red from the blood being pushed up to my head. Luckily, I remained conscious. When I regained my vision, I was looking up at the palm trees on the base. My #2 man was yelling, "Eject! Eject!" I knew the seats in those days weren't much good below 2000 feet, and since I was at about 100 feet, I stayed with the jet and wrestled to regain control of it. Passing over the beach, I looked back and saw the area of impact where #4's jet had hit the water. He never got out. I began a slow climb, and #2 and #3 joined up on me, #3 still flying with three feet of his wing missing. They informed me that my tailpipe was smashed and the whole aft end of my jet was bent upward, akin to the spine of the plane being broken. I was basically a piece of metal going forward. Only a Grumman product would still be flying in that condition. I eventually discovered that I could control the plane above speeds of 220 knots, and ended up making a 225 knot landing at Kingsville.

INTRODUCTION

We lost a good man that day, and there are no words to describe how we all felt. A new pilot volunteered to take his place. The team went on.

To have been selected to form, train, and lead such an elite organization as the Blue Angels offered me a great sense of pride, honor, and unparalleled challenge. When first formed, we could have never guessed that the team would still be here, 50 years later. But we always set extremely high standards for ourselves. In doing so, a unique bond was created between team members, regardless of rank or rate. This deep sense of pride was truly the heartbeat of all of our thoughts and actions. It showed in every element of our performance.

Today, aircraft are sleeker and much faster, yet much remains the same. It is still pull, turn, and roll. Refinements and innovations have continued throughout the years, but the standard of excellence has not wavered. The spirit we felt in those early days continues with the members of today's team. Their position in the sky has been hard earned. When I look at the proud young men called Blue Angels now, I see the faces of those who were there in the beginning: "Wick" Wickendoll, Mel Cassidy, Al Taddeo, Robbie Robinson, and Billy May. Together we set the standard that has been handed down to each team. The performances of the Blue Angels continue to dramatically portray the conviction, skill, and courage of the Navy fighter pilot. It was not equaled 50 years ago. It has been widely imitated. It remains unequaled today.

In the following pages of this book, you will gain a rare and penetrating insight into the Blue Angel experience. With accuracy and candor, Brian Shul tells the story of the "Blues" in pictures and words from a position that few have ever shared. This book has been long overdue. It was worth the wait.

I shall eternally be thankful and proud to have had the opportunity to be the 1ST BLUE, and to share, from the beginning, the Blue Angel experience.

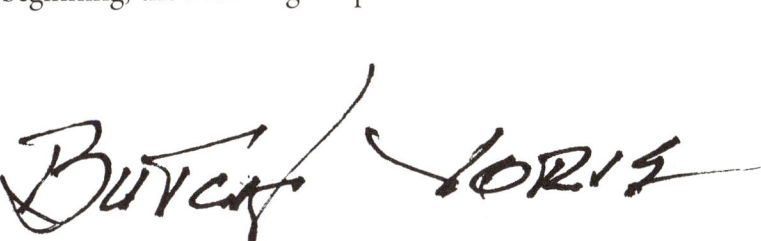

Butch Voris

R.M. "BUTCH" VORIS, CAPTAIN, USN (RET)

Commemorating their 50th year of excellence

The Blue Angels
United States Navy Flight Demonstration Squadron

1996

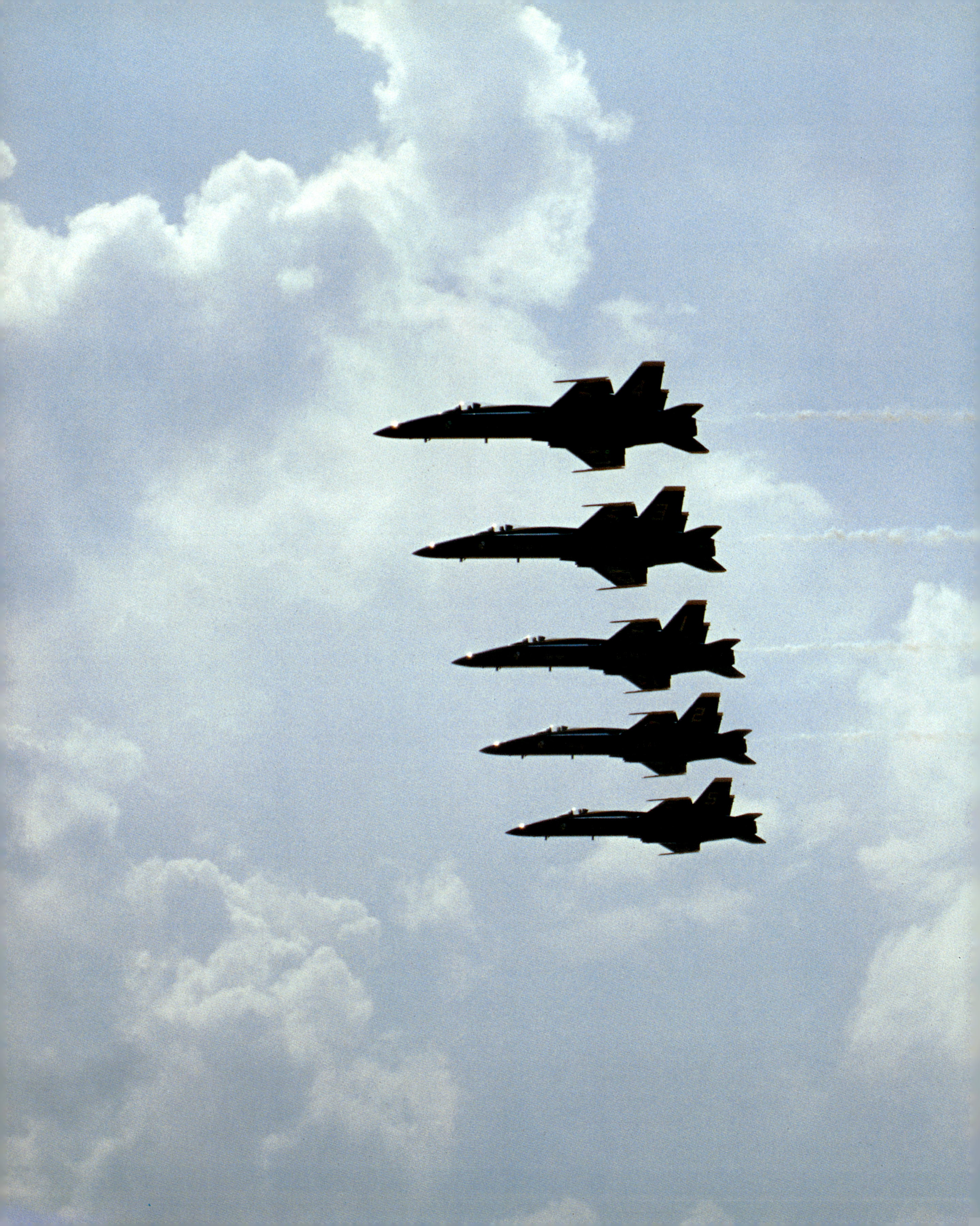

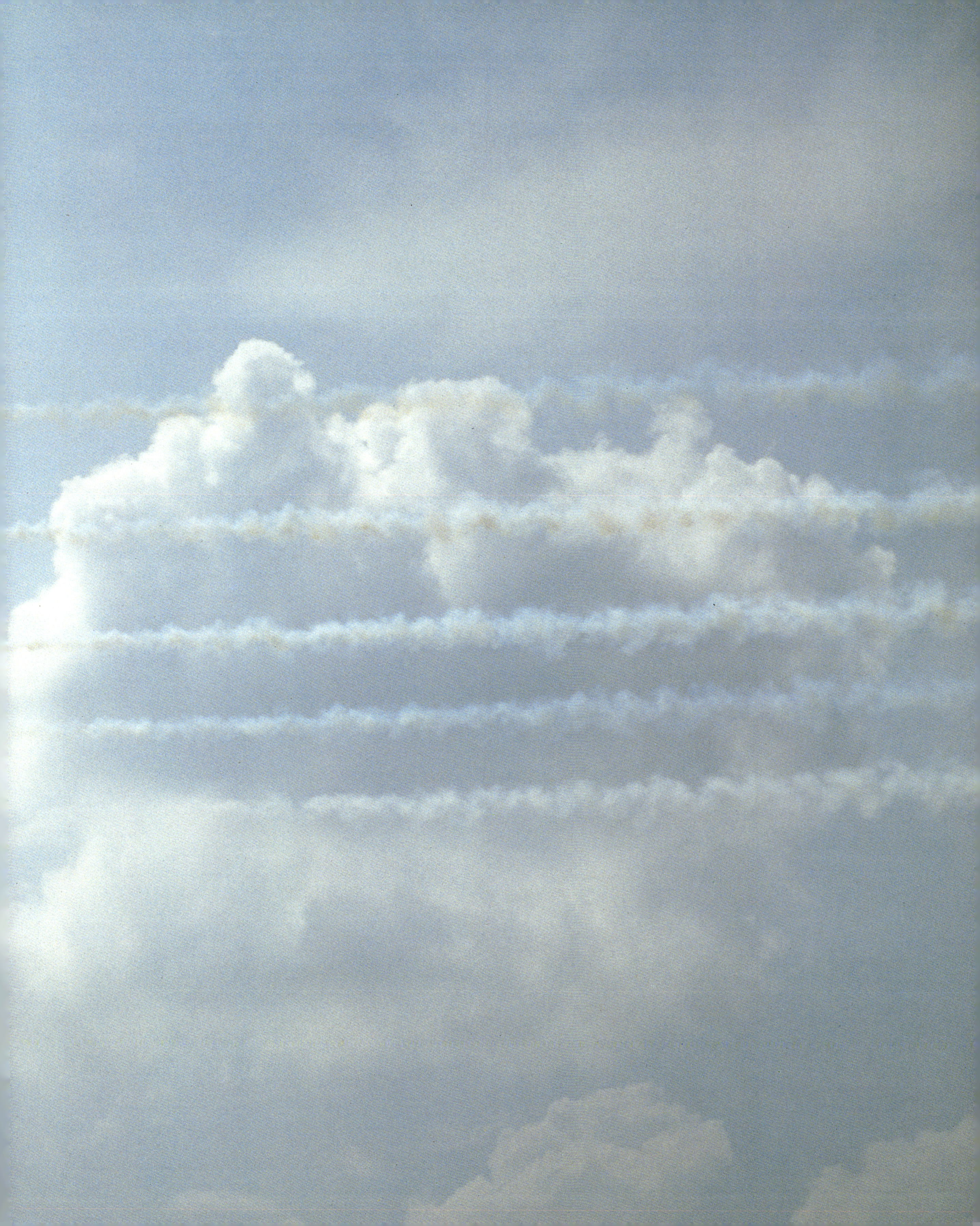

22

BLUE ANGELS *A Portrait of Gold*

Often different generations of aircraft will meet on the air show circuit. A vintage 1930s Boeing N2S Stearman, a primary trainer for many early Navy flyers, buzzes a quiet F/A-18 Hornet.

1 The Living Legend

The mere mention of the name "Blue Angels" amongst aviation enthusiasts easily arouses attention and often sparks spirited discussion. Someone will recount a story, or two, of when they had witnessed the team's daring flight exhibition, and were either highly impressed or slightly frightened, or both. Comparisons will likely follow from those who have seen other military flying teams. Often they will proclaim the "Blues" (as the Blue Angels are referred to by those in the business), as the best they have ever seen. Regardless of preference, everyone seems to have a strong opinion about this Navy flying team, and at the very least, nearly everyone seems to have heard of them.

The oldest of our nation's military flight demonstration teams, the Blue Angels over the past 50 years, have gained an aura of respect and recognition from the public, granted to very few military organizations. Even amongst other pilots, there is a measure of honest admiration that is as impressive as it is widespread.

There are several widely acclaimed military aerial demonstration organizations around the world, but none are more instantly recognized than the Blue Angels. There are other teams in brilliantly painted jets that bring aerial precision to an art form, but most spectators agree the Blues are the most exciting to watch. The British, French, and Italians all field teams with more jets in close proximity to each other, yet the most popular team in all of Europe today remains the US Navy's own Blue Angels. The Canadians do things truly impressive with nine small Tutor jets in unique formations. However, after watching both them and the Blues perform, what most viewers will remember is just how tightly the larger and more powerful blue Navy Hornets flew that diamond formation.

There is a prevalent feeling among air show enthusiasts, triggered with the knowledge that the Blue Angels are coming to town, that seems to transcend all reason and any regard to aerial proficiency. Seemingly, the other teams are simply excellent; the Blues are dynamic, even scary at times, and are in your face with maneuvers others don't even want to try. Regular jets parked on the ramp are pretty neat; seeing the blue jets with the gold lettering parked on your ramp is stimulating, and means your air show somehow really rates. The other guys are professional; the guys in the blue jets are professional, and very cool. The air show, on its own, is entertaining; with Blue Angels on the program, it becomes electrifying.

There is little logic involved in these emotions. In reality, there is little difference in skill level and professionalism amongst the world's premier military flying teams. Yet, what is undeniable is the pervasive high esteem and widespread adoration the air show public singularly exhibits for the Blue Angels. Are the Blue Angels really better then the rest, or do their fans simply think they are? Perhaps a little of both, though neither may be as important to their success and popularity as the Navy system that spawned them, where uncompromising excellence is measured through performance.

The story of the Blue Angels is as much the story of the exploits of naval aviation in three wars, as it is about air show performances. Gaining an understanding of the Blue Angel mystique as it is today requires first an understanding of the basic Navy fighter pilot's approach to flying and the environment that helps to shape him.

This relatively small group of naval officers train to fly and fight from the rolling decks of aircraft carriers. They train realistically, knowing they may have to fight someday, and they accept that nothing of value comes easily. Not much else in their line of work does either. While at sea, they will frequently be far from command centers or supply lines, and must ensure mission accomplishment with only what is at hand. They have learned to do much with little. These pilots work together with their shipmates as if their life depended on it, as it may, and within the task force, they become part of an integrated fighting team. They are more directly concerned with daily operations than staff planning. In their pursuit of mission accomplishment, these professionals will be required to make many command decisions, which in the process exercise their abilities to be assertive, flexible, and creative. They relish their independent authority. That the higher command structure encourages and even expects this decision making process, elevates confidence, and capability within the flying units.

Navy pilots accept that their profession is a dangerous one and sometimes people are going to die. They do not use this fundamental fact to curtail training requirements. They cannot afford to. Among other skills, Navy pilots need to maintain carrier landing proficiency, and that never gets easier. They either wash out in training, or get very good at their profession – or they die trying. It is not a business for everyone. They are volunteers, and love their work, even though there is often little that is easy, fun, or glamorous about it. In today's world, littered with the waste and wreckage laid down by the political processes of lessening standards, these folks can only be called politically incorrect.

There are those who do not understand this approach to flying and have been critical of it. They are usually people who have never launched from the deck of a carrier or landed on one at night, in deteriorating weather, low on fuel. However, they are often the same people quick to expect success from our naval forces when conflict is necessary. And Navy pilots throughout their history have delivered, forging their hard earned aerial victories in combat, as solidly as the steel hulled ships that have carried them into battle. From Midway Island, to the Battle of the Coral Sea in Hellcats over the Pacific, to jet carrier operations in the Panther during the Korean War; from Yankee Station in the Gulf of Tonkin where Navy Phantom pilots rewrote the book on air tactics over the skies of North Viet Nam, to the Mediterranean and the flaming of Libyan MiGs by F-14 Tomcats, this bold group of flyers has met every challenge thrown their way, and continues to do so today. It was from this proud tradition of prodigious expectations and stellar accomplishments that the Blue Angels were born.

When men of this mettle are asked to form a flying demonstration team, and allowed room to maneuver toward mission accomplishment, they will likely yield remarkable results, and could be very exciting to watch. And so, it is not surprising that they did; and they are. These are people who thrive on challenging themselves. Once a Navy pilot has survived the ordeal of night carrier operations, he feels as if he can do anything, and nothing in Blue Angel history suggests that team members have thought any other way.

The very beginnings of US Navy aviation date back to 1911 (the first Marine Corps pilots flew one year later in 1912) and aerial showmanship seems to have been a Navy tradition long before the Blue Angels ever took to the sky. Prior to the team's inception after World War II, several other Navy flying acts had performed for the public in a variety of special occasion shows. As early as 1928, a three plane team called the Sea Hawks dazzled the crowd with their formation precision by flying three Navy Boeing F2Bs actually tied together in flight. Most of the early flying teams were short-lived though, and in 1946 Admiral Nimitz officially sanctioned the US Navy Flight Exhibition Team.

The Navy knew well the importance of its air arm, and wanted to keep it in the public eye. This display was not only for political reasons, but for economic reasons as well. The Navy recognized a need to stem the mass exodus of flyers from the service after the war.

Living and working on board an aircraft carrier breeds a certain kind of "can-do" mentality. For those who fly planes aboard the carriers, this concept is often elevated to "can-do anything." The directive to form a Navy flying team was received on 24 April 1946. On 15 June, Lieutenant Commander Roy M. "Butch" Voris climbed into his F6F Hellcat at Jacksonville, Florida, and proceeded to lead two wingmen and a solo pilot through the first public showing of the Navy's fledging demonstration team. In a mere seven weeks, Lieutenant Commander Voris had drawn up a complete show routine, hand-picked his pilots, meticulously trained them in flight, and completed the first public demonstration without a hitch. In true Navy fashion, this small group of pilots forged ahead confidently. Unafraid of failure, these men simply tasked themselves as necessary to succeed in their mission. This was little different from anything these men had been doing for the previous four years as Navy combat pilots.

No one better personified this spirit of tenacious preparation for mission success than the new team's leader, Butch Voris. As a Navy pilot, Voris entered World War II flying the Wildcat, a plane quickly found to be inferior to the Japanese Zero. During the air battle over Guadalcanal, his aircraft was shot down. Undaunted, he returned to fly the newer Navy Hellcat. He went on to become a Navy Ace in the Pacific Theater, finishing the war with eight aerial victories. He was awarded the Distinguished Flying Cross three times.

Lieutenant Commander Voris realized he was breaking new ground when asked to head up a flying team that would represent the entire US Navy. Voris relished the opportunity. The Navy offered the team little guidance, and even less support at times, but every man on the team recognized the Navy expected much from the team's performance. Because they were writing their own script as they went, these pilots couldn't realize that they were actually laying a foundation upon which future Blues would build a tradition second to none in the aerial demonstration business. Years later, Voris remarked, "We thought the team would probably last about three months."

From the very beginning, the team had a degree of autonomy that allowed them to function as they deemed necessary. With a maneuver as poised as any diamond roll, the team was able to bypass official protocol and garner the name Blue Angels for themselves.

After only a few months in the Hellcat, the team began flying the more powerful F8F Bearcat. This plane was the first to form the famed Blue Angel diamond formation. With that massive propeller up front, the diamond could not yet attain the tightness which would later become a staple of Blue Angel performances. However, the Bearcat did introduce the diamond roll and loop to the public.

Though the aircraft were far less sophisticated than today's jets, early Blue Angel performances did not lack flair and excitement. Though only 17 minutes long, the entire show could be kept within the confines of a 7000 foot runway, dynamically conducted between 2800 and 10 feet of altitude. Pilots in the audience flinched as they watched the three planes in the "V" formation roll on their individual axis with very minimal clearance from each other. Looking back, Butch Voris would later say, "That really was quite sporty."

Additional drama was added to the early shows as postwar audiences were entertained with the simulated shoot-down of a "Japanese Zero." The Zero was actually a Navy SNJ trainer, painted in Japanese markings. Near the end of the Blue Angel performance, the "Zero" would attack the Hellcats, only to be quickly outmaneuvered and "shot down." From the back seat of the SNJ, a dummy pilot, complete with parachute, was thrown from the plane. Once on the ground, the "enemy pilot" was quickly surrounded by a platoon of Marines as the "Zero" disappeared over the horizon.

Once, while the Blues were performing a rehearsal show for a group of Navy dignitaries, the parachute static line broke as the dummy pilot was thrown out of the SNJ, causing it to fall well off its mark. There was more than one wide-eyed VIP as the uniformed mannequin came crashing to the concrete, a mere 15 feet in front of the seats. After landing, Lieutenant Commander Voris was directed to report to the reviewing area. He was positive his days as Team Leader were over. The admiral simply said, "Butch, quite impressive show, yes, quite impressive. May I make one suggestion to the routine – I think maybe that dummy can be dropped just a little further out from now on."

BLUE ANGELS *A Portrait of Gold*

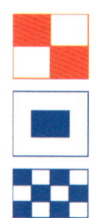

A formation of Blue Angel time machines: F6F Hellcat, F8F Bearcat, F9F Panther, F9F-8 Cougar, F11A Tiger, F-4J Phantom II, A-4F Skyhawk II, and the current F/A-18 Hornet

With the increased speeds of the Bearcat came new dimensions of risk in the area of G loads on the aircraft. In September of the team's first year, solo pilot Lieutenant Robbie Robinson became the first Blue Angel fatality when his aircraft suffered structural failure in a high speed dive.

The team continued on and quickly realized the need for a winter training season. Finally, this training season was instituted by the end of the 1947 air show season. Limits were also set for length of tour with the team. Two years became standard due to the physical demands of precision flying and the continuous stress of nonstop travel.

When the Blue Angels received their first jet aircraft in 1949, they actually continued flying shows in the propeller driven Bearcat, while simultaneously checking out and flying formation in the new F9F Panther jet between shows. Due to the very different control feel of both aircraft, this required intense concentration and dedicated effort by all. These two traits would continue to be the foundation of Blue Angel performances throughout their history. With the advent of the jet age, the SNJ and its "Japanese Zero" theatrics were retired from the show, and the team concentrated on expanding its repertoire of maneuvers.

In the summer of 1950, the Korean War necessitated the Navy transferring Blue Angel pilots back to combat duty. The whole team was reassigned to VF-191, thus forming the nucleus of the squadron known as "Satan's Kittens." The squadron was highly experienced, and had an outstanding combat record. Sadly, Lieutenant Commander Magda, former Blue Angel Leader, fell to enemy fire over northern Korea, becoming the first Blue to be lost in combat.

The Korean War could have easily marked the end of the Navy's young flight demonstration team. But in an era of increasing need for jet pilots, the Navy could not ignore the tremendous impact the Blue Angels had on the public at large. Once again, naval air power was proving itself in battle, and needed highly motivated young men to tackle the challenges of jet carrier operations.

In only four years of existence the Blue Angels had exceeded everyone's expectations. The team had performed before 14 million people gaining widespread recognition and popularity. As a result, many high ranking Navy officials began to see the team's value, not only in terms of recruiting potential, but as a morale builder in the service as well. In 1951, while fighting continued in Korea, the Chief of Naval Operations issued a directive to reactivate the Blue Angels.

With all the pressures emanating from reforming a whole new team in the shortest amount of time, the obvious choice for Team Leader was Butch Voris, who was then serving a tour with the Navy staff in Washington.

The Blues were once again gracing the skies over America, and they dynamically brought the jet age to millions of people in the early 1950s. In 1954, the first Marine pilot joined the team. Marine fighter pilots had written an illustrious chapter in military aviation during World War II and the Korean War, and had become an integral part of the Marine Corps' fighting force. A separate flying team for the Marine Corps was impractical. Due to their close operational ties with the Navy, the Marine Corps was allotted one demonstration pilot slot on the Blue Angels. This practice continues on to this day. Additionally, Marine aviators would go on to fly Blue Angel transport aircraft that are so vital in carrying men and equipment to each show site. Today, Marines also occupy several ground support positions with the team.*

In 1955, the team moved from Whiting Field to their present day location at Pensacola Naval Air Station in Florida. However, the single most important move that would thrust the Blue Angels into the public's consciousness occurred two years later.

In 1957, the Blue Angels made a switch in planes from the Cougar to the newer F-11F Tiger jet. The Tiger was a sleek Grumman jet that gave the Navy its first supersonic fighter. Like most jets of its day, the Tiger was somewhat underpowered, and never received great acclaim in its role of fleet defense. Eventually, the plane was replaced with faster, more capable jets. What the

---

*General references to Navy aviators in the text include Marine Corps pilots.

aircraft lacked in tactical performance, however, it more than made up for in graceful lines, and gained its greatest fame in its 11 year service as a Blue Angel. The team had considered the A-4 Skyhawk, an aircraft that would later prove to have great longevity. However, the team preferred the Tiger jet because of its afterburner. (Ironically, Blue Angels would fly the Skyhawk some 16 years later.) With a mixture of beautiful imagery laid across purposeful sound, the Tiger jet, in the hands of Blue Angel pilots, won the hearts of all who witnessed its performance.

The aircraft seemed perfectly tailored for the Blue Angel diamond, and aesthetically enhanced each maneuver. It was a perfect match, and during an era of unprecedented peacetime air shows, more people would view the team in this plane than in any other. The Blues would gain international fame in this jet, which many people today often recall as their first Blue Angel memory. Thus, with the Tiger, the Blue Angels entered the era of supersonic jet teams, and before crowds of unparalleled size, began to solidify their stance as the most highly acclaimed and visible flying demonstration team in the world.

People who knew little about the intricacies of formation flying found utter enjoyment in the beautiful symmetry of those blue and gold Tiger formations. In 1965, the Blue Angels were invited to the Paris Air Show and stunned a record crowd with their aerial artistry. In a rare display of appreciation, a very discriminating reviewing stand audience gave the Blues an unprecedented standing ovation.

In 1968, the Tiger jet was retired from Blue Angel service, having long since been withdrawn from the regular fleet. This marked the end of 22 consecutive years in Grumman aircraft for the Blue Angels. The team had come of age while in the F-11F, and the plane will forever hold a special place in the team's proud history. Today, Blue Angel Tiger jets can still be seen, proudly guarding the entrances to both the Blues' home base at NAS Pensacola and their winter training site at NAS El Centro in California.

When the Blues replaced the venerable Tiger jet with the F-4 Phantom II, it marked a new level of air show intensity for both the performer and spectator. Whereas the Tiger had once embraced the crowd with its symmetry and grace, the F-4 now muscled its way into the crowd, and shook them with a strength never before seen in the air show arena. The Blue Angel performances in the mighty Phantom II still rank today, for many people, as the most exciting jet demonstrations ever witnessed. They were also the most difficult and dangerous to fly.

The F-4 was more powerful and had greater speed than its predecessor, but it was more difficult to corral into the confines of an aerial routine. Performing in Canada, a Blue Angel solo pilot in the F-4 actually got supersonic inadvertently during a crossing maneuver, much to the chagrin of air show officials and the exhilaration of the crowd. The demands on Blue Angel pilots were severe in putting four Phantoms together in that famous blue diamond. The plane was very sensitive to the disturbed airflow emanating from those around it and the wingmen were constantly having to push the plane inward toward the Leader in order to stay in position. Extremely pitch sensitive at high speeds, and not particularly forgiving at slow airspeeds, the heavy F-4 demanded the full attention of the pilot at all times. There was never any problem gaining the full attention of the spectators at these shows either, as it was truly an awesome spectacle to witness.

The F-4 era, though short-lived, brought the Blue Angel mystique to new levels of danger and excitement. The crowd became more emotionally involved. With eight afterburners roaring at them on takeoff, they had little choice. This was the largest of all Blue Angel planes, and as such afforded the crowd an opportunity to occasionally detect the movement of the planes within the diamond formation. The spectator no longer viewed the formation as a solid entity, now more aware of the superb airmanship and elements of danger involved in the process. Even pilots in the audience could get sweaty palms watching this show. One Air Force official, after viewing the Blues in the F-4, was heard to remark, "Every time I turned around, someone was inverted."

THE LIVING LEGEND   29

The Blue Angels have been seen by more people the world over than any other flight demonstration team. Given the relatively small size of the Navy's air arm, the popularity of the team worldwide is astounding.

BLUE ANGELS *A Portrait of Gold*

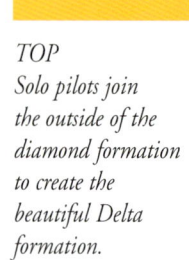

TOP
Solo pilots join the outside of the diamond formation to create the beautiful Delta formation.

BOTTOM
The Boss and #4 are inverted in one of the Blues' signature formations, the famed Double Farvel, seen here from the #3 position.

The Blue Angels' reputation as the hottest team in the business echoed across airfields as sharply as the distinctive sound of F-4s in afterburner. Spectators were prone to think, surely, these men must possess superior skills to perform such mastery with this beast of a jet. While others were certainly just as talented, the Blue Angels seemed to perform their routine with a certain amount of flair, long one of their trademarks. As if flying the jets in close formation through a myriad of difficult maneuvers wasn't enough, who else would put the Leader upside down in the diamond and call it the Farvel? The same team that later decided they could fly both the Leader and #4 inverted in diamond formation and call it the Double Farvel. Crowds were left breathless, often shaking their heads in amazement. The legend grew. Over 400,000 people showed up at Dulles International Airport one afternoon just to view the Blue Angel performance in the F-4. What the Tiger jet did for the team's exposure, the Phantom did for its notoriety in performing *the* show to see.

This type of acclaim is hard earned by Blue Angel pilots. They take a very serious and professional approach to their flying, spending many arm-numbing hours honing their skills to a fine edge. But it is not without a price. Though the team flew the F-4 for barely five years, three team members were killed in aerial mishaps during that time, one being a Team Leader. Six Phantoms were destroyed in the process. These numbers were unacceptable by any standards, and the team was forced to regroup and eventually switch to a new plane. Finally, a growing concern for safety and high operating costs forced the Phantom out of the air show business, and it was retired from Blue Angel service. Those five years in the F-4, though, were the most unforgettable in Blues' history and helped solidify the team's reputation as the world's most exciting aerial demonstration.

The early 1970s marked the end of the big air show era as budgetary constraints forced military teams to cut back dramatically on their air show schedules. The A-4 Skyhawk II was the new plane for the team and it was a good compromise. What it lacked in muscle, it made up for in agility with an excellent thrust to weight ratio. Though small, it was far more economical and easier to maintain than its larger predecessor.

The Blue Angels maximized the little Skyhawk's performance, and continued to impress the public with their flying skills by demonstrating such extraordinary maneuvers as the six-plane Delta formation landing. For thirteen years the "Scooter" would remain with the team, eventually bringing the Blues into the era of high technology planes.

The Blues celebrated turning 40 with the transition to the F/A-18 Hornet, and have continued to fly it well over 10 years now. In the Hornet, the team has an enviable blend of power, size, and agility. Impressive at both ends of the speed spectrum, the F/A-18 allows the team to perform show maneuvers that would have been unthinkable in the older planes. The rugged Hornet comes from the same McDonnell Douglas lineage which delivered both the Skyhawk and Phantom, possessing the best attributes of both, and much more. As such, the F/A-18 gives the Blue Angels an exciting dimension to their performances reminiscent of earlier days when the team replaced the stubby Cougar jet with the supersonic Tiger.

Though modern technology has made today's jets safer and relatively easier to fly than their predecessors, it has also given them unprecedented maneuverability, resulting in greater physical stresses on the pilot in the cockpit. Putting the F/A-18 through today's Blue Angel demonstration, Blues pilots must push themselves to the edge of endurance to maximize their aircraft's performance, and their own.

Furthering the Blues' reputation as being the toughest team in the business is the longstanding Blue Angel tradition of not wearing G-suits during their performances. Remarkably, this practice continues today, despite the physically punishing maneuvers of their F/A-18 routine. Due to the unique way Blues pilots position themselves in the cockpit to compensate for a heavily down-trimmed stick, there are functional reasons for this practice. Add to that the constant 30-35 pounds of added stick force each pilot must oppose throughout every maneuver, and there is little doubt that these are some very tough pilots. While some may consider the absence of G-suits a bit unsafe in lieu of the Hornet's G capabilities, Blue Angel pilots regard it as

BLUE ANGELS *A Portrait of Gold*

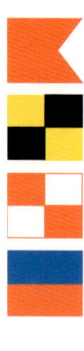

The solos, #5 and #6, complete the very demanding Double Tuck-Over Roll. Entering show center inverted, they will fly a section 270 degree roll. Seen here, nearly halfway through the maneuver, it is as difficult to perform as it is exciting to watch.

THE LIVING LEGEND

simply another challenge in their pursuit to be the best. Accordingly, they prepare themselves both mentally and physically for the intense strength their performance demands. Regardless of the explanations, there is no doubt that today's Blue Angel performances without a G-suit makes for some intensely physical flying. That no other jet team flies this way today has only served to enhance the Blue Angel mystique.

In spite of fiscal constraints, minimal support from the Navy at large, and exhaustive air show restrictions, the Blue Angels continue to excite crowds across America and around the world. In 1992, the team brought their blue Hornets to Moscow. They were the first team from America to perform for the Soviets, engaging in a most memorable cultural exchange with Russian pilots.

With a plane that can "roll your socks down" and "turn a square corner," the Blue Angel show today is as dynamic as it has ever been, and turning 50 years old in this business has been no small feat.

Since Butch Voris led that first team off the ground in 1946, the Blue Angels have flown over 3500 demonstrations. In the process, they have carved themselves a unique and unforgettable place in this nation's aviation history. With great pride and much sacrifice, 181 men have represented the best of Navy/Marine aviation as Blue Angel pilots in the team's first 50 years. In their pursuit of excellence without compromise, 22 gave their lives while serving as Blue Angels.

Though much has changed since blue Hellcats dazzled post World War II audiences, so much of today's Blue Angel demonstrations are indelibly linked in purpose and performance to those early teams who set a simple standard to be the best. To many, they still are. And for many, this team still carries an aura of surreal greatness that has been as much a part of Blue Angel history as the very real pilots and planes themselves. While spectators love and appreciate other teams, the Blue Angels inspire awe. While many teams put more jets in the sky, none fly them harder and closer than the Blues. Wherever planes are flown, very few people have not heard of the Blue Angels.

There is no denying the mystique, which to this day surrounds this most famous of military flying teams. To appreciate the Navy tradition of excellence that has spawned it, one need to look no farther than the faces of today's team members. Regardless of the team observed, the current Blue Angels proudly represent those who have gone before them, forming a living link to the naval traditions and uncompromised standards that have molded a team heralded the world over.

To fully appreciate the Blue Angel experience today, one would need to observe team members personally at their place of work, and witness the unceasing effort required to produce such a remarkable aerial demonstration. To best understand what it means to be a Blue Angel, one would have to spend an entire air show season living, traveling, and, most importantly, flying, with the world's most recognized team. You, however, may simply turn the page....

BLUE ANGELS *A Portrait of Gold*

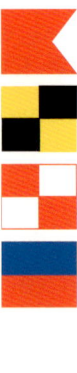

TOP
Prior to the plane taxiing, smoke is checked on the ground. It is simply a crude blend of oil dumped directly into the exhaust, and controlled by a switch in the cockpit.

BOTTOM
On takeoff roll, #4 sits on the outside of the diamond until airborne, at which point he will slide into the slot position behind the Leader.

THE LIVING LEGEND

35

TOP
The very graceful diamond Tuck-Under Break, requiring precise timing and consistent roll control by everyone.

BOTTOM
Over the top in the diamond Dirty Loop. The Leader is the only one who will not lower his tail hook for this maneuver, in deference to #4's close slot position.

BLUE ANGELS *A Portrait of Gold*

Just moments after takeoff, the diamond enters the show opening loop. The deep stack of #4 on the Leader is evident in this view, a trademark of the Blue Angel diamond.

37

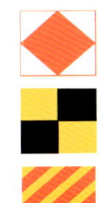

The diamond Echelon Roll, a maneuver the books say shouldn't be done. With all three jets lined up on one side of the Leader, #1 will begin a turn into the formation. As seen from the #3 position, #2 and #1 are well into the roll. Any movements from the front of the formation will ripple down in increasingly dangerous increments.

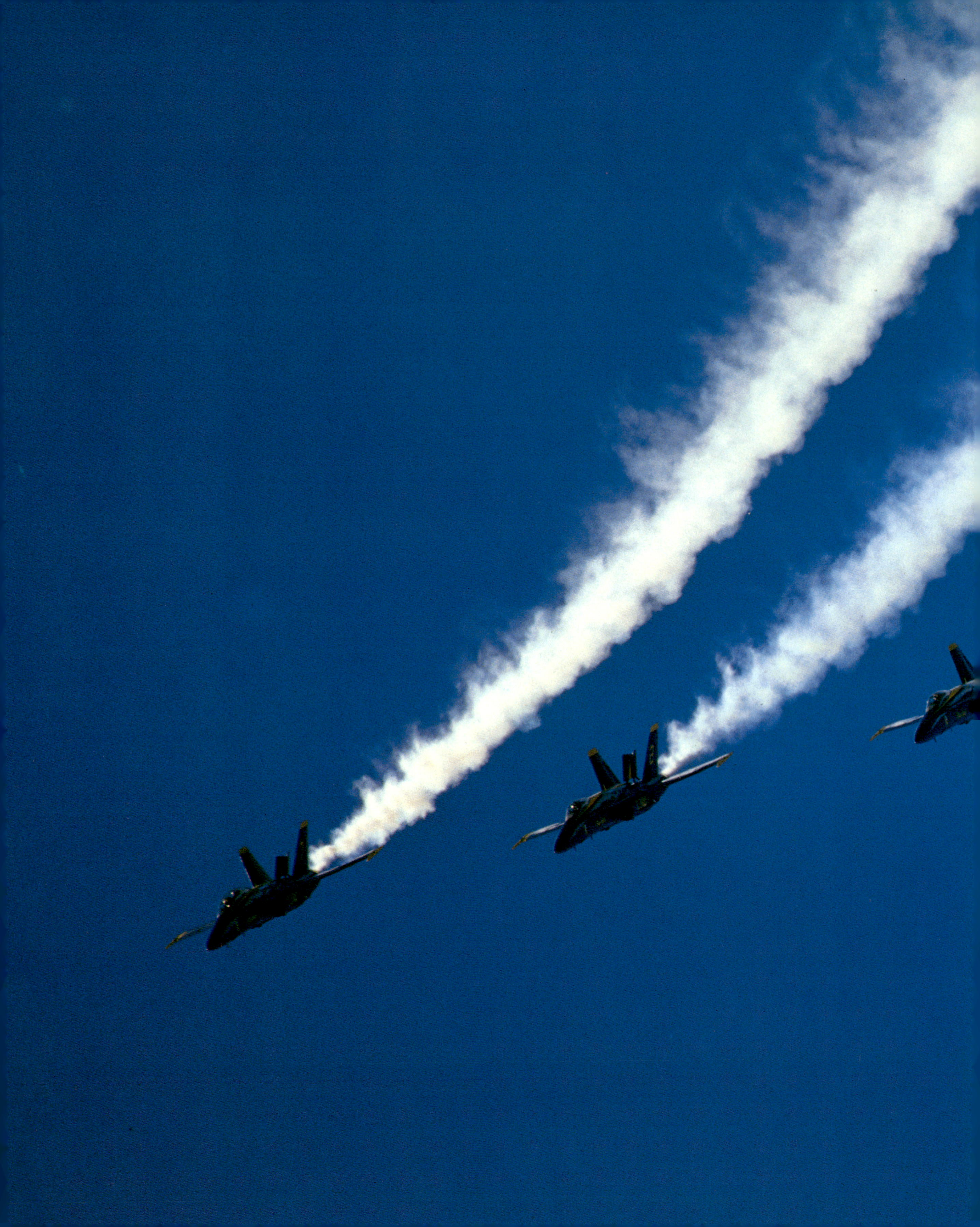

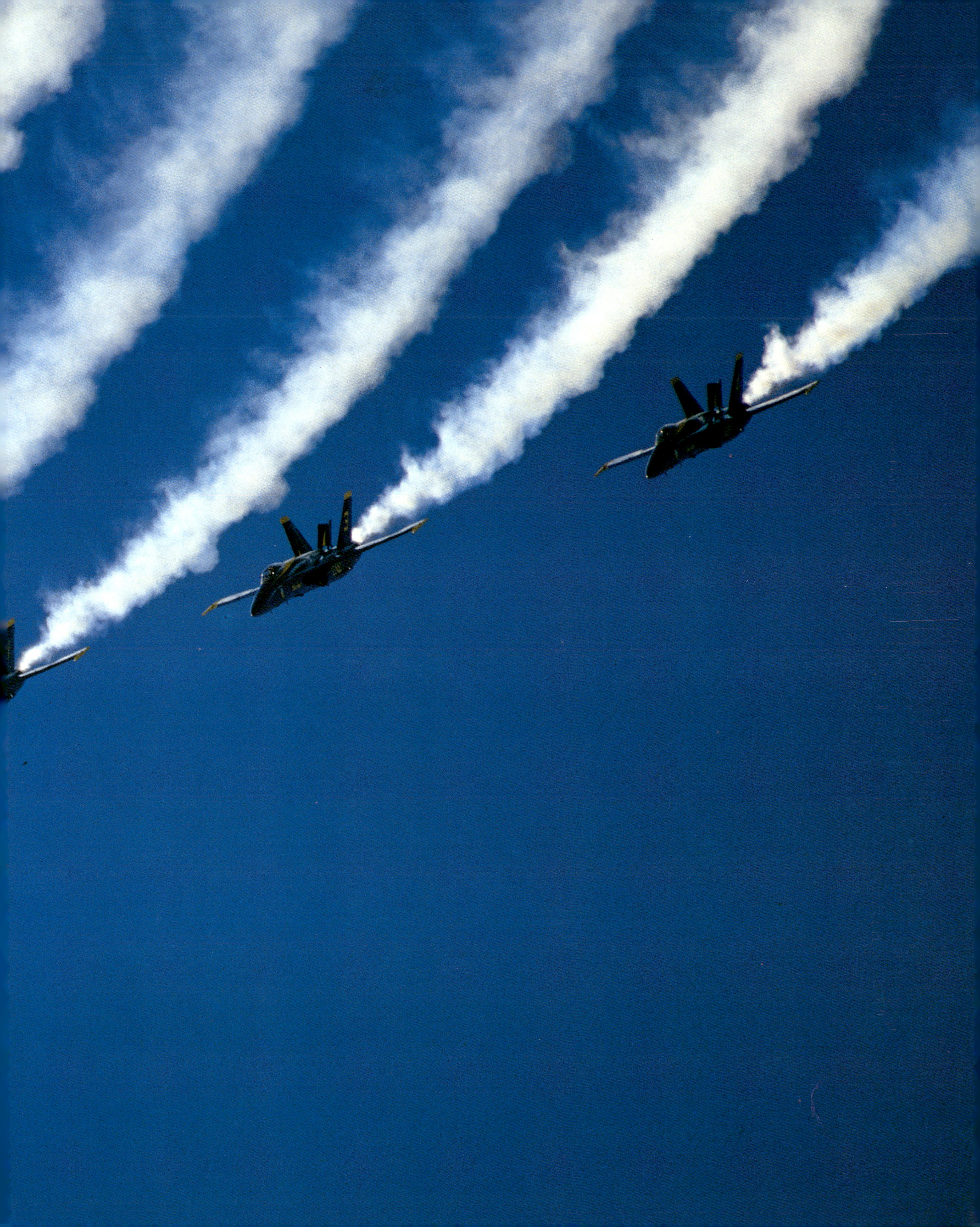

BLUE ANGELS *A Portrait of Gold*

Blue Angel formation flying begins on the ground, with minimal wing tip clearance while taxiing out.

2 The Rites of Spring

Luke Air Force Base, Arizona

✦✦✦✦ It is only April, and the air feels like midsummer on the ramp at Luke. Even though it's 98 degrees, the heat has not diminished the crowd. More than 60,000 folks in the greater Phoenix area swarm to the Air Force Base to view this Navy team. As I view the blue Hornet jets from across the taxiway, the rising heat waves make them appear as if they are baking on the shadeless concrete.

Yesterday the team flew a practice show over the field and while taxiing out, the Boss blew a nose tire for no apparent reason other than the heat. With impressive quickness, the maintenance crew changed the tire at the end of the runway and within minutes the show went on. Today, maintenance personnel, congregating around the jets, remark about how hot their shiny black shoes are, roasting in the bright sun. They enjoy coming to Air Force bases to perform since it usually means excellent support services, and a chance to see new places. The Air Force base likes it as well, because the team's presence boosts crowd attendance greatly for this event that comes early in the show season.

Briefing Room

✦✦✦✦ Before the briefing, the pilots sit around a large conference table eating lunch and chatting amongst themselves. At the end of the table rests the video monitor that will be used extensively for the review of the show tape during the debrief. Every show and practice flight is taped, and every tape is meticulously reviewed by the team in order to improve their performance.

The six demonstration pilots, the Narrator, and Events Coordinator will occupy seats at the table, while chairs along the walls will seat the additional support officers attending the briefing. Conscientiously, I try to memorize everyone's name, but soon discover my efforts are wasted.

Listening to team members converse, I notice they use nicknames when they talk to one another. These names represent their call-signs in flight, and are used for all radio communications. So complete is this process that rarely does one hear or use actual names throughout an entire tour with the team. While there is usually a story behind each nickname, squadron etiquette dictates that you ask only the person whose name you are questioning in order to get the straight scoop on its origin. The #3 pilot is called Snooze. He points out that if you really want to irritate someone on the team, refer to him by his official rank and complete name. It's a sure sign that he is in some sort of trouble.

The Leader is simply Boss. This is a tradition handed down from earlier teams. Flying the right wing in the diamond, in the #2 position, is Lawman. Snooze is on the Boss' left wing in the #3 spot. Dino flies in the #4 slot position. Hoops is the lead solo as #5, and Timber complements him as the opposing solo, #6. The Narrator, #7, is known as Daddy, and works closely with the Events Coordinator, #8, called Surge. With only a couple of exceptions, all of them are in their thirties, and are married with young children. In their profession, they represent an upper level of jet fighter experience.

Surveying this group of professional flyers, there is a sense that this is an all-star team, made up of some of the finest pilots in the entire Navy. Aside from their positions as naval aviators, this group of young men closely resembles any random collection of all-Americans from across this country. Although they depict a diverse mix of military experience, they merge together as a team, forged by the commonality of their respective skills as naval aviators.

A tall, slender man sits studiously at the end of the long table, intently studying a field diagram of Luke Air Force Base. Of the 5000 hours he has spent flying Navy jets, 3000 of them have been in the F/A-18. He was among the very first Navy pilots to test the Hornet's mettle, taking it into combat during the Libyan crisis in 1986. Again, four years later, he flew strike missions in support of Desert Storm. For his heroism in the air, this quiet, unassuming man was awarded the Distinguished Flying Cross. Confident in his abilities to meet any challenge, he now embraces perhaps his most difficult test of all —that of serving as Leader of the Blue Angels. As Boss, he sits at the very forefront of the Navy's most visible squadron, a position only a chosen few have held. As the Boss looks up from his diagram for a moment, his expression is as intense as one before any combat mission.

The rest of the team is a microcosm of Navy fighter pilots everywhere, many of them having been instructor pilots with the fleet. Lawman and Snooze make up the wing positions of the famed diamond formation. Lawman is the sole Marine demo pilot. Formerly, he flew Harriers before coming to the team and saw action during the Gulf War. Prior to becoming a Blue Angel, Snooze was one of only a handful of Navy F/A-18 tactical demonstration pilots performing individually at air shows around the country. Dino flew A-7s initially, then Hornets, and now has many hours as an instructor in the F/A-18. He is no stranger to flying demonstrations, having also performed them in Hornets before coming to the Blues. Both solo pilots are graduates of the Navy's Top Gun School in the F-14 Tomcat. Hoops returned to the school, flying the F-16N as an adversary pilot, and Timber has taken the F-14 to a variety of air shows as a tactical demonstration pilot. Daddy was an instructor pilot in the A-6 Intruder, and Surge served as a Naval Flight Officer aboard the S-3, participating in one of the first ever S-3 bombing missions over enemy territory during Desert Storm.

Though they all now wear the same uniform, these men's backgrounds are as unique as their different sobriquets. They hail from Vermont and North Dakota, from Missouri and Arizona, and from Kansas and Pennsylvania. They received their college degrees from such schools as the University of Connecticut, Bates College, Northwest Missouri State, and Arizona State University, and their majors were just as diverse – Agriculture, Economics, Criminal Justice, Oceanography, and Aviation Administration. Boss is the only graduate of the Naval Academy among them.

There is an unspoken understanding that their positions on the team were not simply awarded, but hard earned over much time and many hurdles. Seeing them together now, they are equal; they are Blue Angels, and wear no rank on their shoulders. Though they are an honest representation of fleet pilots everywhere, there are few flyers anywhere who will work as hard this summer as these men in the blue flight suits.

Amidst hurried eating, the men in the briefing room continue to talk and kid with each other. The nicknames also seem to extend to the staff officers. The Maintenance Officer, or M.O., is forever referred to as Mo. Lieutenant Commander Ottery, the Administrative Officer, is known as Otter. The team's Public Affairs Officer, Lieutenant Kirby, answers to Cubby; and Joe, one of the team's Marine C-130 pilots, has become simply Heyjoe. No one seems exempt, and within the team the names are a symbol of acceptance and camaraderie, becoming somewhat official in an unofficial sort of way.

The pilots were in a joking mood prior to briefing for today's flight, all except for Lawman. He is a very friendly guy, but has that serious look of someone in grade school who this morning has to make a presentation in front of an assembly. He is very quiet, speaking only when spoken to directly. He is the new guy in the diamond, and this is his first show season with the team. He has weathered the intensive trial of winter training season, but will spend most of his first show season really learning his position. Normally, there would be two new diamond pilots, but the Boss and Snooze are in their second year and Dino is in his third, so Lawman sits alone at the table as the new guy. Because of this status, he will routinely endure the most scrutiny and criticism in the debriefings. It is a ritual they have all been through and has nothing to do with personal feelings. Rather, it is a process necessary to ensure the precision required to fly one's position properly. To these people, "properly" is akin to

THE RITES OF SPRING 43

Solo pilots will not just fly opposing passes during a show, but will join for several dynamic maneuvers in section, a two plane formation. This requires quick rendezvousing behind the crowd in order to be set for the start of these maneuvers. In this photograph, the solos complete the Section High Alpha, a maneuver which sees them fly as slow as 110 knots.

perfect. There is little or no room for error when putting four jets together with less than three feet of separation.

Lawman is one of the easiest people to talk to on the team, and he is easily liked by all who meet him. While Snooze and Dino kid each other over a Gatorade, and the Boss munches on a sandwich, Lawman sits motionlessly and silently. He stares intently at the airfield diagram before him, and reviews the notes from yesterday's debriefing. Outside, his assembly waits.

Like all good fighter squadrons, the Blue Angels adhere to the basic philosophy that sarcasm and humor are essential to healthy squadron life. To be kidded heavily is a good sign, and denotes acceptance and strong self-esteem within the group. And it makes people laugh, something very important in the midst of the stress that this team routinely endures. I am treated only with politeness, and I know well the trust and respect that effective pointed squadron humor requires is only earned with this group, not given.

The two solo pilots are discussing sports. Snooze points out that the solos sit at the end of the table, apart from the rest of the guys, because they aren't quite diamond pilots, and have for some time suffered from "diamond envy." Timber retorts that the diamond maneuvers are just "filler" between the real show, the solo performances. Dino looks around the table in a playful mood. He spies Lawman engrossed in his notes. In a couple of hours, the show will be over, and Dino will likely be debriefing Lawman unmercifully for some aerial miscues. It's Dino's responsibility and Lawman would want it no other way. Dino has been there. He started with the team on the Boss' left wing as #3, and now is in his second year as the slot pilot. He directs his stare at Lawman and for no apparent reason, bellows in a slow deep voice, "LAW-MAN." Then he just gives Lawman that surreptitious grin that Dino does so well. Lawman acknowledges the reference briefly, and continues reading. Dino turns to me and says with a serious scowl, "Lawman's not allowed to smile, he's a first year guy. I'll tell him when he can smile." Then that grin again.

Flightline

✦✦✦✦ For this point in the year, the show goes well. Performances early in the season can sometimes be rough, as the team doesn't start to really jell until several months into the season. During yesterday's practice over the field, Lawman fell slightly out of position during the Diamond Dirty Loop. This was not a problem, since he performed the proper clearing move that takes him slightly out of the formation for that maneuver.

This is a very critical movement as each plane in the diamond has a certain amount of airspace they may clear. Once a pilot clears from a maneuver, he is out of it altogether. He's either all the way in, or all the way out: there is no in-between. The worst sin is not falling slightly out of position, but rather clearing to the wrong airspace, as that could be the first step toward a midair collision. Lawman revealed today that, many times during winter training, it was more difficult to learn the clearing avenues of each different maneuver than it was to learn the maneuvers themselves. Lawman looked good in the Diamond Dirty Loop today. Usually, though, in a 42 minute show of this nature, there will likely be some other area requiring closer scrutiny in the debrief.

✦✦✦✦ After landing, the pilots look exhausted standing in the afternoon heat, and they heartily gulp down ice water brought by the maintenance van. Shortly thereafter, they move to the waiting crowd, and stay for nearly half an hour, patiently signing programs thrust toward them from every direction. While finishing up the autograph session, Snooze flashes his wide smile at one admiring 10 year-old and asks if he liked the show, and gets an emphatically positive response: "Well, great, that's the main thing, pardner." And so it was.

Redmond, Oregon

✦✦✦✦ The team has just completed the big weekend show at El Toro in southern California, where over 1.4 million people saw it perform. They are worn out from the numerous "commits" (official social commitments) and other demands that a show of that size entails. The small town of Redmond, Oregon, nestled near the peaceful Cascade Mountains, is a welcome change of pace for the team. For many of the 9000 inhabitants of Redmond, this will be their first Blue Angel show. For most team members, this is their first visit to Oregon.

No commits are scheduled on the mornings of show days in order that the pilots may relax. Some play a round of golf at the resort hosting them. Others swim or jog. Doc, the team flight surgeon, got up early and climbed a nearby mountain. Their free time is a precious commodity for they will spend most of the year giving their time to others, whether during a show, signing autographs, posing patiently for pictures, talking with the media, visiting schools and hospitals, or being the guests at any number of dinners and special events.

The Briefing

♣♣♣♣ The team briefs today at the terminal of Redmond's regional airport. They require a room free from disturbance, preferably with a large table, and air show officials are normally quick to comply.

During the briefing, the interaction between the Boss and #4 provides a deeper understanding of the unique makeup of the diamond. While the Boss is the squadron commander and leads the team, calling out the maneuver changes over the radio, it is #4, the slot pilot, who runs the formation and calls those changes. As such, he will also run the debriefing, rather than the Boss, since he flies in the optimum position to best observe what everyone is doing. He has to be able to not only fly his own plane, snugly wedged between three others, but to take notice of what everyone else is doing in order to instruct them afterwards in how to make it better. Due to the inherent difficulty of trying to perfect maneuvers in close formation, everyone is going to make mistakes. Often they are small ones, indiscernible to the spectator; sometimes, they are not so small, and one of #4's most important tasks is helping to ensure that the latter are the rare exception.

The slot is a difficult position and flown by pilots only in their second year. The slot pilot is the heart and soul of the diamond. Like the catcher in a baseball game who works the pitcher and positions players, #4 watches the Leader's every move, and moves people in and out as necessary. He will remind the Boss if he's missed a call, watch the overall safety of the formation by keeping an eye on altitudes and hazardous obstructions, and adjust his own position to make the formation look symmetrical to those on the ground. Sometimes, he may sound like a coach in an effort to settle everyone down during a particularly difficult day. If either wingman drops out with an aircraft malfunction, it is #4 who will move up into the vacant position on the Boss' wing and fly the remainder of the show from there, a position he may not have seen for many months.

The slot pilot forms the backbone of the formation. He must not only handle the flying, but be a good instructor on the ground as well. When he speaks, he commands the attention of all in the diamond, including the Boss. Sometimes he has to be the "bad guy" and bluntly issue some not so favorable comments on the performance. It is necessary in a business where complacency can kill and lack of total proficiency is unacceptable. #4 can swing the mood of the team easier than anyone else, and he must delicately balance his comments in a room full of strong egos, so as not to negatively affect the general mood of the team. A slot pilot once remarked, "some days it is more important that we get along than that we fly well".

Dino seems made for the slot position, and it is difficult to imagine him anywhere else. It is not so difficult to imagine him as a wide-eyed little kid of eight, gripping the stick, and straining to see over the instrument panel during his first Piper Cub flight across the Missouri countryside. Though he loved flying from the first, he nearly didn't get to fulfill his dream, until he found that he could apply for Navy flight training during his sophomore year in college.

From the T-28 to F/A-18s, Dino worked with the same intensity he displayed as an eight-year-old who didn't want to relinquish the stick. Like most young Navy pilots, he originally viewed the Blue Angels as a gifted group of "golden hands", able to fly a routine he could probably never perform as well. Dino has come a long way and now deftly handles the intricacies of his slot position with such a smooth style that one might forget just how much hard work and training preceded it. He, in fact, admits that he wanted to fly the slot from the beginning, and like the slot pilots before him, relishes this most challenging of positions as the best place to fly.

Dino is tall for a fighter pilot at 6'4", and walks with a slow gait. He is somewhat of an enigma, ranging freely between soft-spoken sincerity, and cold, blunt honesty, bellowed unmistakably to the point. At times, he is a good actor and often, in the team's best interest, appears more intense than he really is. Flying in the diamond for a third consecutive year can be fatiguing, and there are times when the boys cut him a wider path than normal. You know where you stand with this man, and that is how it needs to be in a formation that is uncompromising in its structure and unyielding in its quest for the elusive perfect performance.

In a rare moment of reflection, Dino has said, "No one, except the guys who have done it, really understands just how difficult this is. The Navy, in general, has no idea how hard this is, and considers it somewhat of an 'easy' tour, since it's shore duty. In addition to flying this incredibly unforgiving formation, you have to be 101% all the time while on the ground, in everything you do. That little kid in the wheel chair who's waiting to talk with us doesn't know that we might have almost killed each other up there, and we just have to set that aside, because the most important thing we do is to portray a positive role model to those people out there. I take that very seriously." Listening to Dino speak, you know he does.

Dino has earned his credibility, and well understands the wall that new guys on the team hit during winter training season, when they begin to feel like they can't perform even the most basic maneuver correctly. Asked to stay on for a third year, Dino can still recall his first: "I thought I was fairly good, but when I got here I found out that I couldn't do anything right from basic formation to marching. There is a higher level of performance required here, and on this team it is proven performance which counts most."

Dino comprehends the intricacies of the formation, and, more importantly, can instruct them, better than most ever have. On the surface, it seems at times as if he is constantly hammering Lawman in the debriefs. Yet it was Dino who gave him the best instruction during winter training, helping Lawman get over some tough hurdles.

Sitting in the slot, Dino gets the big picture of the formation, and seems to have even a bigger picture under control when he says, "I wasn't the greatest pilot when I arrived, and I won't be when I leave this team; there's always some guy out in the fleet that's better. I'm just a regular guy working hard." It's a motto shared by the others on the team.

Unhappy with the team's past couple of performances, Dino gives a little talk before the briefing today. He also reminds them of the higher density altitude at Redmond, which when coupled with the heat, will negatively affect the thrust of their jets. The Diamond Dirty Loop is removed from today's performance because of this factor. From his deep #4 position, Dino flies a slightly wider arc in the loop than the rest of the diamond, and his jet would likely run short of thrust at the slow airspeeds, with the gear hanging, at the top of that loop.

The Boss is not exempt from #4's critique and comments, and professionally acknowledges that he has been a little inconsistent while rolling inverted to set up the Double Farvel maneuver, and will work on that today.

Conspicuously absent at all times are excuses and argumentative remarks from any of the pilots. Striving together, for perfection, they truly understand and adhere to the concept of "team".

Redmond Airport

✦✦✦✦ The small town of Redmond bulges with people from all over the state who have come to witness the Blues over Oregon. The local population has grown by a factor of seven as the small regional airport is overrun with spectators.

The heat and turbulence across the mountainous terrain cause increased difficulties for the pilots, as there is more bouncing occurring in the diamond than is comfortable. To the crowd, it is simply a magnificent performance by this team, so seldom seen in this part of the country. For the diamond pilots, it was a rough ride as 40 tons of blue metal precipitously bounced together through invisible patches of clear air turbulence. As one Blue Angel pilot put it, "Sometimes we hold hands with Death up there, and just have to keep a firmer grip than it does."

As the pilots climb down from the cockpits, the stress of the past 40 minutes is evident on their faces. The solos are soaked with sweat and chat briefly amongst themselves at the water wagon (maintenance van). They discuss today's Double Tuckover Roll, one of the most difficult maneuvers they fly. No other team even does this maneuver. Flying across show center in close formation at 200 feet, both inverted, rolling 270 degrees simultaneously, is a bad place to find a pocket of turbulence. They found one.

Snooze and Lawman got close today during a formation change. Uncomfortably close. Sipping water calmly now, with a slight grin, Snooze remarks to Lawman, "Did you see that big blue thing next to you? That was my jet." They both laugh, but it is the hollow laugh of men who, for just a moment today, felt the tugging of Death's grip in their hand.

Regardless of how exhausting a show it might have been, the team is always able to set it aside once the autograph session with the crowd begins. Smiling and chatting with the people as they sign programs, these men show little evidence of the intense and draining moments they have just endured in flight. To a man, they all admit that the very best and most rewarding part of their job is talking with and portraying a positive role model to the young kids in the crowd. This is not always easy to do, but they take it as seriously as their formation, and watching them laugh and converse with the spectators, they seem momentarily far removed from the fury just witnessed overhead.

NAS Corpus Christi

✦✦✦✦ Corpus Christi represents command headquarters for the Blue Angels as they are officially a part of the Navy Training Command. Residing at Pensacola, the team is most often allowed to conduct squadron business on their own, with little micromanagement from the command staff.

The first thing most noticeable about Corpus is that it is humid. Very humid. Even the seagulls seem to fly a little slower here. On the first show day, the team made a valiant effort to perform in the face of low clouds, reduced visibility, and a thunderstorm in the vicinity. Immediately after takeoff, and prior to flying any show maneuvers, the team performed a weather check of the local area. Much to the disappointment of the crowd, the team landed moments later, with the knowledge that conditions were unsafe for any demonstration flying. The Boss hated having to make that decision, but knew he had no choice, as safety is never something compromised by this team.

The weather dictates what type of show the team can fly. They can perform a flat show (no formation rolls or loops, flat passes only) when clouds are too low for vertical maneuvering, a low show (formation rolls but no loops) when the ceiling is slightly higher, and the high show (formation rolls and loops) when weather conditions are generally clear. For any show, there must be a minimum of 3 nautical miles visibility for the team to perform.

On the second show day, the weather is only slightly better and the team flies a flat show. There is only one show day left, and the team would really like to be able to do a high show for their headquarters base, especially with such a large and enthusiastic turnout from the local populace. The weather seems to have a pronounced effect on the team. As they leave the briefing room for their cars, they note the worsening skies overhead and seem to be in a bit of a flat mood themselves.

By their very nature however, this team is unable to remain flat for very long. On the ride back to the hotel, Snooze and Dino reminisce about their early days in the training command as brand new student pilots. Dino received his wings at Corpus and nostalgically points toward the water and the USS Lexington in the distance, where he made his first carrier landings. Snooze recalls the "horror" of that first time when it was "just you, no instructor, just you and the LSO on the deck." Snooze could've joined the Air Force, but thought it looked exciting landing on carriers, so he chose the Navy. He admits to thinking he was really somebody when he took that first trap. They talk with the unbridled enthusiasm of young ensigns as they recall their first introduction to night carrier operations. The stories are a combination of comedy and horror. Snooze willingly relates, "When I finally got it down on the deck that night, my knees were shaking so much I could hardly hold the brakes." Dino laughs, but tells his own stories with equal superlatives and candor. Having just watched these men fly through marginal weather conditions, unwaveringly fixed in the #3 and #4 points of the diamond, it is hard to imagine them as nervous, inexperienced students. Observing Snooze tucked in, a mere couple of feet from the Boss' wing in the Diamond 360, is to witness the embodiment of rock-solid formation, many memories removed from early days of shaking knees. The stories continue, and for miles, two Blue Angels talk freely of the trials of a past, which helped forge their skills, and put the Blue Angel crest on the flight suits they now so proudly wear.

✦✦✦✦ Finally, on the last day of the Corpus show, the weather breaks enough for a high show. Everyone is happy. The crowd, some of whom have shown up on all three days now, even break into hearty applause during some of the maneuvers.

Everyone on the team is anxious to get home, but the weather which pounded the Gulf Coast of Texas, has now moved eastward toward Pensacola, so there is a three hour delay.

Nothing seems to come easy in this business. After spending hours getting tons of equipment loaded into the C-130 cargo plane, Blue Angel maintenance and support personnel finally take off for home, only to experience an engine malfunction over Louisiana, necessitating an emergency landing. Instead of greeting their families in Pensacola after a long weekend, 40 Blue Angel support folks spend Sunday evening discussing lodging requirements with one surprised duty officer manning base operations at NAS New Orleans.

At Pensacola, six blue jets have landed safely, and in a matter of hours, another week of Blue Angel business will commence in preparation for the next show.

THE RITES OF SPRING

The Blue Angels are the only demonstration team to perform the diamond Dirty Loop. Muscling the jet through a loop with the gear hanging is a testament to not only the pilots' skills, but the brute force of the jet as well.

BLUE ANGELS *A Portrait of Gold*

TOP
Crew chiefs await the pilots prior to a demonstration, and become air show spectators for a fleeting moment.

BOTTOM
The guys prior to the march-down. From the left: Boss, Lawman, Snooze, Dino, Hoops, and Timber.

THE RITES OF SPRING 51

BLUE ANGELS *A Portrait of Gold*

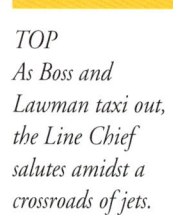

TOP
As Boss and Lawman taxi out, the Line Chief salutes amidst a crossroads of jets.

BOTTOM
Timber stands on his tail with his show opener, displaying the incredible climb capacity of the Hornet on takeoff.

THE RITES OF SPRING

TOP
Dino, the tallest member of the team, tightens his straps before engine start. Once the show starts, there is little time to adjust anything, and cockpit strap-in is a meticulous process for all.

BOTTOM
Looking beneath #3's jet from the slot, Hoops is seen in the Delta formation over the little town of Redmond, Oregon. This is not the solos' most favorite formation to fly, as they spend a majority of their time perfecting their solo maneuvers and find the constrained life of a wingman a radical change of pace.

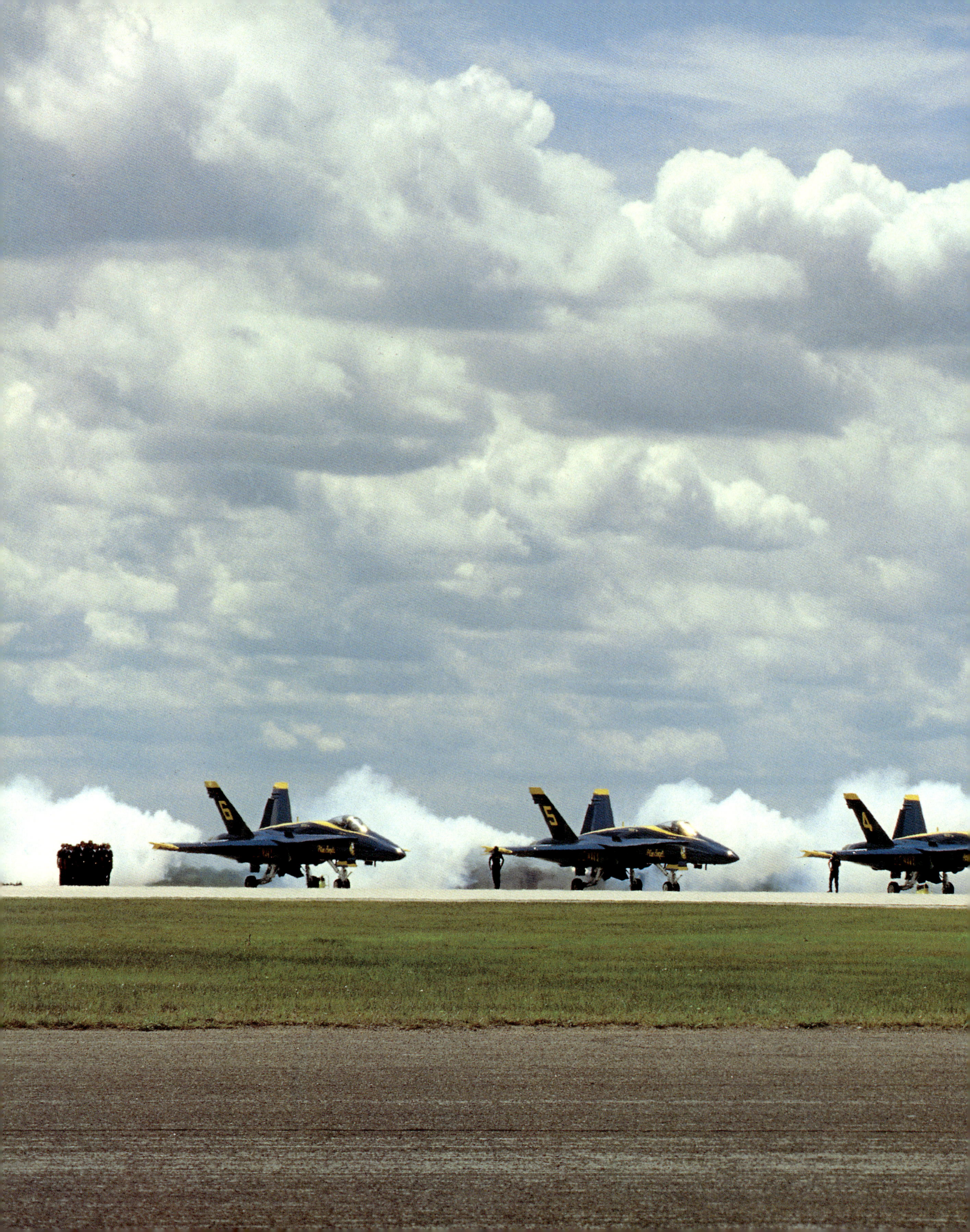
6
5
4

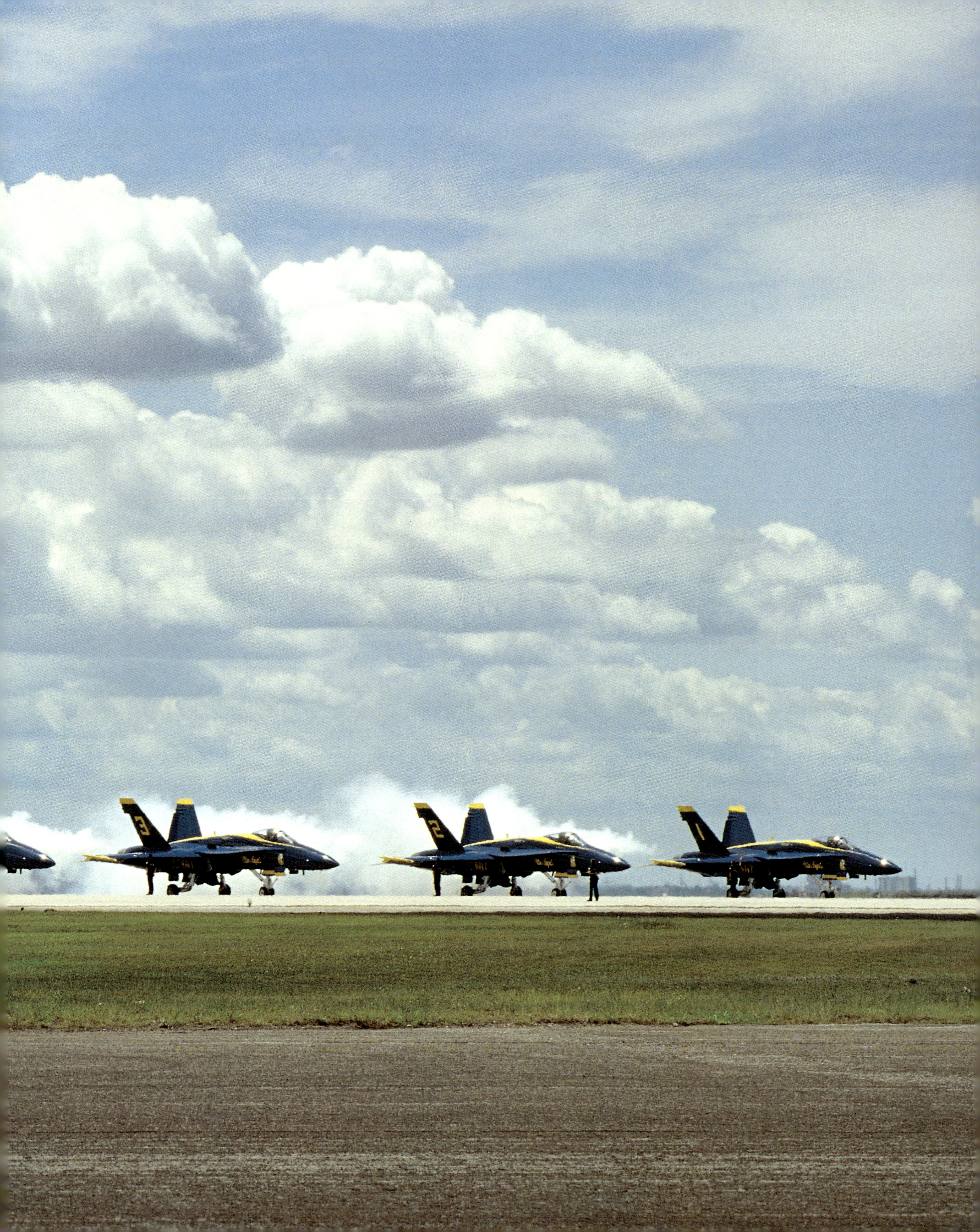

56

BLUE ANGELS *A Portrait of Gold*

Since altitude is not a factor during performances, the Blue Angels use a boom mic instead of an oxygen mask. This arrangement is more comfortable on a constantly sweating face during the high G maneuvering, and also means that there is one less thing needing servicing on a daily basis. For long deployments at high altitude, masks can be easily fitted to the helmets.

3 Home Base

NAS Pensacola, Florida

✦✦✦✦ Situated in the Florida panhandle, Pensacola Naval Air Station is home to the Navy's most recognized squadron. Consistent with Navy convention, the Blue Angel facility at Pensacola is nothing fancy, and except for the title "Blue Angels" painted on the building, it blends in almost unnoticed at the end of the airfield. There is little here that suggests the facility houses a world famous demonstration team. Sharing a building and hangar space with the local jet training squadrons, the Blue Angels operate in relative austerity at their home base. Since it is the Navy way and they are accustomed to it, this condition is of little consequence to the team. To them, it's always better than being out at sea.

As the week begins, the squadron is busy with a variety of activities. A light rain is falling and maintenance people are towing several planes into the hangar for touch-up painting. One jet is due for a phase inspection and is placed on jacks, so that all of its vital components can be removed, cleaned , and inspected.

This means one of the spare planes will be repainted with a corresponding tail number and become one of the six planes that make up the demonstration. It is Lawman's jet. On top of everything else, he will now be adjusting to the different feel of flight controls in another jet. Although these differences are subtle, in the delicately intricate world of flying close formation throughout a broad spectrum of speeds, they are felt instantly by the pilot whenever an aircraft change is made. Numerous flights will occur before the new feel becomes normal, and any other changes will see the process repeated.

Keeping six planes ready for the team every day is a demanding job for the Maintenance Officer, and Mo approaches his job with an enthusiasm and proficiency that he expects from every one of his support people. Blue Angel flying is hard on the jets from a maintenance point of view. While the planes are structurally tough enough to endure where the pilots take them, subsystems within the plane occasionally suffer from the constant G loads. Often, it is the small problems which cause the most concern, since they are the toughest to track down and fix. Until corrected, they can ground a plane.

Mo's job is further complicated by the fact that the Navy does not give the Blue Angels new jets to fly. They are not even relatively new. The F/A-18s which so proudly bear the Blue Angel colors, are the fleet's oldest Hornets, representing some of the earliest models of F/A-18s delivered to the Navy. Certainly, the Navy's best interest is served by keeping the newest and most updated planes with the fleet, and team pilots heartily concur. But it is a testimony to Blue Angel maintenance expertise and ingenuity that six aging Hornets are able, on any given day, to fly a show that stresses the aircraft to their design limits.

Mo is assisted by a highly experienced cadre of maintenance supervisors who oversee just under a hundred specialists, mechanics, and crew chiefs. Additionally, two technical representatives from McDonnell Douglas are assigned to the team. Representing a combined experience of 50 years of technical expertise, they will travel with the team to every show, spend the entire winter training season with them, and assist maintenance in any way they can.

As is the Navy way, no one on the flightline has just one job, but will be tasked to broaden their career field expertise with learning other specialties while serving with the Blues. About half of the maintenance personnel will accompany the team during each road trip.

Watching Blue Angel maintenance in action, their efforts exemplify the credo of "doing more with less."

Even the Maintenance Officer wears two hats. Prior to any demonstration flying, his first responsibility is to deliver six good jets to the pilots. He entrusts his line chiefs with a great deal of responsibility and won't hesitate to exercise his authority to "own any Hornet part in the US within 24 hours." He ensures that routine inspections of jets will affect the pilots only minimally, as he tries to deliver the same bird to each pilot for each show: "The solo pilots are the most particular about which jet they fly, and I try never to swap out the Boss' jet if it can be helped."

During a flight demonstration, however, Mo becomes the safety observer, standing out at the communications trailer with direct comm to the Boss at all times. Mo is also linked by radio to the tower during a show, and takes ownership of the airspace while the Blues are airborne: "If anything moves out there, I'll know it, and I won't hesitate to stop a show if I see an unsafe situation."

Mo's job on the team is more complicated than any normal squadrons' M.O., but like everyone else with the Blues, he thrives on challenge. Beginning his naval career in the enlisted ranks, Mo can empathize with his young troops who, not too far removed from high school, are tackling the complexities of today's F/A-18: "With a sophisticated array of black boxes, this is a very smart jet – some days, smarter than we are." Mo progressed from enlisted mechanic to eventually qualifying for a commission to ensign, and has earned a degree in professional aeronautics from Embry-Riddle Aeronautical University. Traveling with the team over 300 days a year, causes him to reflect that "it's a testimony to my guys' perseverance that we can get it all done." At times, Mo will receive the wrath of disgruntled pilots who occasionally need to vent their frustration over a sick airplane. He will take the responsibility, unquestioned, and before coming down too hard on his people, he remembers that they are all pitching in and "would rather be here doing this job than anywhere else in the world." Mo recalls that he never responded well to people shouting at him when he was a young seaman on the line, so he tries to avoid it with his men.

The typical weekly routine for the Blues begins with a no-fly day on Monday. Tuesday and Wednesday are practice days when the team will fly the show profile. On Tuesdays, the show is flown over the field and small numbers of visitors are invited to watch from a small bleacher section in front of the squadron flightline area. Wednesdays normally take the team over the nearby auxiliary field for a practice. On Thursday, the team will usually be flying to the next show site, returning home Sunday evening.

A small cluster of tourists gathers around the bleachers Tuesday, as the dismal weather has kept some away. The team flies the practice in a light rain. The Narrator, Mo, and Doc, all huddle together at the comm trailer, with no shelter from the rain. With them are a video specialist, an observer with binoculars, and a radio man. All of them are soaking wet.

Like Mo, the Doc performs team duties beyond his primary specialty. During winter training season, the Doc will become well versed in the different maneuvers flown by the team, so that he will be able to critique them from the ground. During every show and practice he will stand, along with Mo, at the comm trailer, aligned with show center, and make notes about each maneuver flown. He'll give his feedback to the pilots during the debriefing, offering a short critique of each maneuver. Though not an aviator, Doc can give the pilots an accurate account of what the maneuvers looked like from a spectator's viewpoint. Coupled with the video tape which is reviewed after every performance and practice, there is not much that is missed by the pilots in critiquing themselves.

Debriefing

✈✈✈✈ Prior to the debriefing, the pilots are concerned that they once again had to fly a low show today. They haven't flown a high show in over a week now due to poor weather conditions, and that is a long time to be away from something requiring daily tuning.

Several monetary fines are levied for various "offenses", which consist of such minor disruptions to team harmony as wearing one's sunglasses when the others weren't, marching out of step, being late, or just about anything else that they can come up with. The fines are kept in a fund which will pay for the squadron party at the end of the season. Hoops informs the Boss that his wearing of a hat this morning, when everyone else wasn't, did not go unnoticed by the team: "That's going to cost you, Boss." As the Boss looked to his right for an out, an unsympathetic Snooze just nodded and said, "Gotcha, Boss."

✦✦✦✦ Doc issues his comments on the Echelon Roll, where the Leader performs a rolling maneuver into the echelon formation. This is a maneuver as difficult to fly as it is to instruct. Dino is not sure Doc's assessment is what was really happening in the air. Careful frame by frame analysis of the videotape shows Dino to be correct. The segment of tape is played over and over again while Dino makes a critical point to Snooze and Lawman about the intricate dynamics of nose position during this sequence. The learning of the maneuvers never ceases.

Snooze remarks that "the most frustrating thing is to see the error when it is happening, and still not be able to correct it." In a performance that covers miles of airspace, it is the correction of inches the team is most concerned with. When asked later if the Echelon Roll is the hardest maneuver for the diamond to fly properly, Dino thinks for a moment, and answers, matter-of-factly, "They're all hard." No smile.

Amidst snacks and bottles of juice, the debriefing continues in an informal atmosphere of videotape review and discussion, punctuated with comments from Doc, then Dino. In the midst of it all, my watch beeps on the hour, with a volume and clarity I had never before noticed. Fumbling for the tiny knob that will kill the beeping on my watch, I finally silence it, and amidst the stares of the others, realize the entire room has also become silent. All seem to be in agreement when Hoops proclaims, "Severe disruption – that'll be five bucks."

✦✦✦✦ Although the flying is completed for the day, the squadron is still busy with maintenance and administrative duties. At the far end of the upstairs hallway is one of the busiest and most important offices in the Blue Angel squadron, the Public Affairs office. Inside, the PA folks are busy preparing signed lithos for presentation to VIPs at upcoming shows.

Cubby, the Public Affairs Officer, is on the phone, beleaguered with numerous requests for the team, most of which are totally out of the question. There seems to be no end to the amount of requests this squadron deals with on a weekly basis. Cubby has to politely explain to a civilian flying organization that the team cannot fly one of its distinguished members. The man is 72 years old. On the other line, an admiral at the Pentagon wants several lithos drawn up for next week's show and has several requests for VIP flights. Another line is ringing and it's a camera crew from ESPN, requesting permission to film the team during a practice at Pensacola. Cubby's desk is littered with a variety of messages on post-it notes. The base museum needs some time to discuss a retirement ceremony, a racing team sponsored in the Daytona 500 is offering team members a chance to drive a lap or two in their car, and some man from town simply wants to know when he can come out to the base and see the Blue Angels fly. While juggling it all, Cubby sighs with pained resignation as he notices a message that's three hours old and simply says CALL WIFE.

On any given week, the Public Affairs Officer (PAO) may have to produce and distribute team lithos; continue work on the Blue Angels Yearbook; issue statements to the media; deal with film crews, magazine writers, and photographers; coordinate VIP visits; meet with celebrities; set up commit schedules; and handle all team requests. Cubby has learned to say "no" frequently, but his ability to assess which requests should get a "yes" is what makes him such a valuable asset to the team.

The Blue Angels convey a very positive image to the public at large, and the PAO is directly responsible for the projection and protection of that image. He is the focal point of the public's contact with the team, and only through the gate of the Public Affairs Office does anyone get to meet or learn about the people on this team. Like a steadfast sentry, the PAO tenaciously

BLUE ANGELS *A PORTRAIT OF GOLD*

Blue Angel facilities at Pensacola are modest, and the base seems to take little notice of their presence. While in their offices, the pilots sit under the constant eye of all Blue Angels past, as pictures of every team grace the walls.

OPPOSITE
The Boss, as seen from #3, providing a stable platform for the rest of the diamond in the Double Farvel.

guards that gate from abuse and misinformation. It is not an easy gate to penetrate. Due to Cubby's tenaciousness and good instincts about who does and doesn't cross squadron boundaries, many on the team have stated that he is probably one of the best PAOs that the Blue Angels have ever had.

The PAO can make or break a team's public image. On a ship at sea, the PAO has some room for mistakes because he is insulated somewhat with an organizational structure that can absorb it. There are no shields with the team; any mistakes in public affairs are highlighted and the PAO is solely responsible, period. He must earn the unwavering trust of the pilots so that they can trust his judgment in the many matters they would never have time to address.

Cubby is interesting to watch at work. He must be polite on the phone and often diplomatic, but always he is firm. He has learned a variety of ways to say "no" to the onslaught of unreasonable requests. He is quick to make a joke, but rarely smiles, constantly aware of the pressure of his post. He must stay at least a month ahead of the team in his mind, and be able to answer correctly anyone's questions about the team.

Cubby had distinguished himself as a PAO on naval vessels prior to coming to the team, but had little or no contact with naval flyers before becoming a Blue Angel. This holds true for many team members, as only a small portion of fleet personnel have direct contact with flying operations. At first, he wasn't quite sure how to take the heavy kidding by the pilots, but soon realized it was a good sign of respect. After several flights in the back seat of the #7 jet, he had a greater understanding for what these men do and how they do it. Cubby has earned the pilots' respect as few support officers have, and it is he who protects the pilots from overzealous autograph seekers and mob scenes at the shows. The kidding directed his way is as unceasing as it is creative. As a junior officer, he gets little help from anyone in the prebriefing bantering.

Cubby has occasionally struck back, and enjoyed his finest "gotcha" on the pilots during winter training. When an admiral arrived from Washington for a visit, Cubby induced him to go along with a little prank. The admiral was to inform the team that due to fiscal restraints, sadly, the Navy had decided the Blue Angels would have to turn in their Hornet jets and start flying the little T-45 Navy trainer hereafter. The admiral willingly followed Cubby's plan and, after briefing a very shocked and somber looking group of pilots, had everyone convinced of the authenticity of his message. No one could believe it, and for two days they lived in stunned agitation. After the admiral flew with the team during a practice, he exposed the ruse during the debriefing, much to the relief of the team. Unfortunately for Cubby, he explained that it was all the PAO's idea.

The eight men sitting around the table all agreed that Cubby had certainly pulled off a good one. When the admiral left, Cubby suddenly remembered some paperwork that needed his attention and hastily excused himself. He never made it to the door. Cubby was carried out of the room via a side window, and locked inside a small barbed wired compound. So as not to let the PAO get too warm in the bright desert sun, the pilots hosed him down thoroughly, and Cubby spent a long afternoon in the mud. They let him out when the sun went down. Cubby hasn't pulled too many good ones lately.

BLUE ANGELS *A Portrait of Gold*

Maintenance is a continuous process for Blue Angel support crews. The fickle weather of the Florida panhandle frequently causes quick changes to the flying schedule, as on this day when a storm cancelled the practice and the jets had to be hangared quickly.

HOME BASE

63

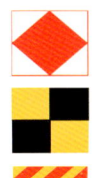

The General Electric F-404-GE engines take a pounding in Blue Angel jets, but deliver extremely reliable performance for the team.

BLUE ANGELS *A Portrait of Gold*

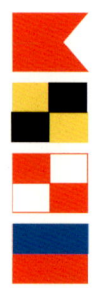

A typical Wednesday practice at Pensacola. Shortly after takeoff, Dino slides into the slot position even as his wheels are still coming up. Twenty minutes later he will slide into his Double Farvel position over the practice range.

HOME BASE

The contrast in the weather typical of the team's two primary locations is evident in these two photographs. Above, the clear skies of their winter training site in California; and below, the Boss checks a grey sky one more time before launching another flat show practice at Pensacola.

BLUE ANGELS *A Portrait of Gold*

Changing from one formation to another involves some of the most dangerous maneuvering to occur within the diamond, and requires precise knowledge of how everyone else will make the move. As the diamond sets up for the Echelon Parade, Lawman is moving slowly into echelon on Boss, and Snooze has agressively taken up his position on Lawman already. Lawman will hear about it in the debriefing.

HOME BASE 67

Flying practices early in the morning make for some interesting lighting, and, on good days, relatively smooth air. A view of Lawman from Snooze's jet, as the diamond repositions and sets up for the Dirty Loop over coastal waters.

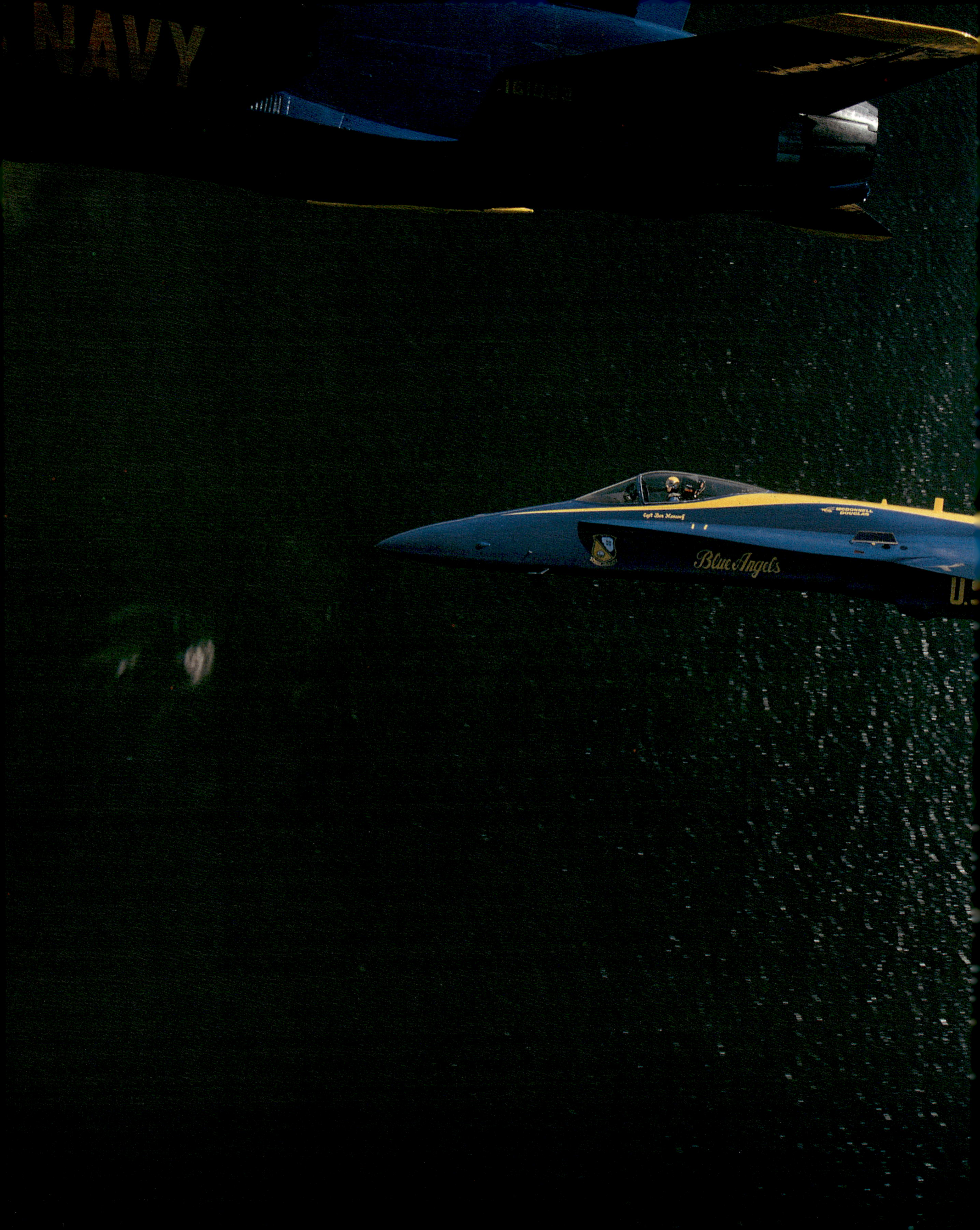
NAVY
McDONNELL DOUGLAS
Blue Angels

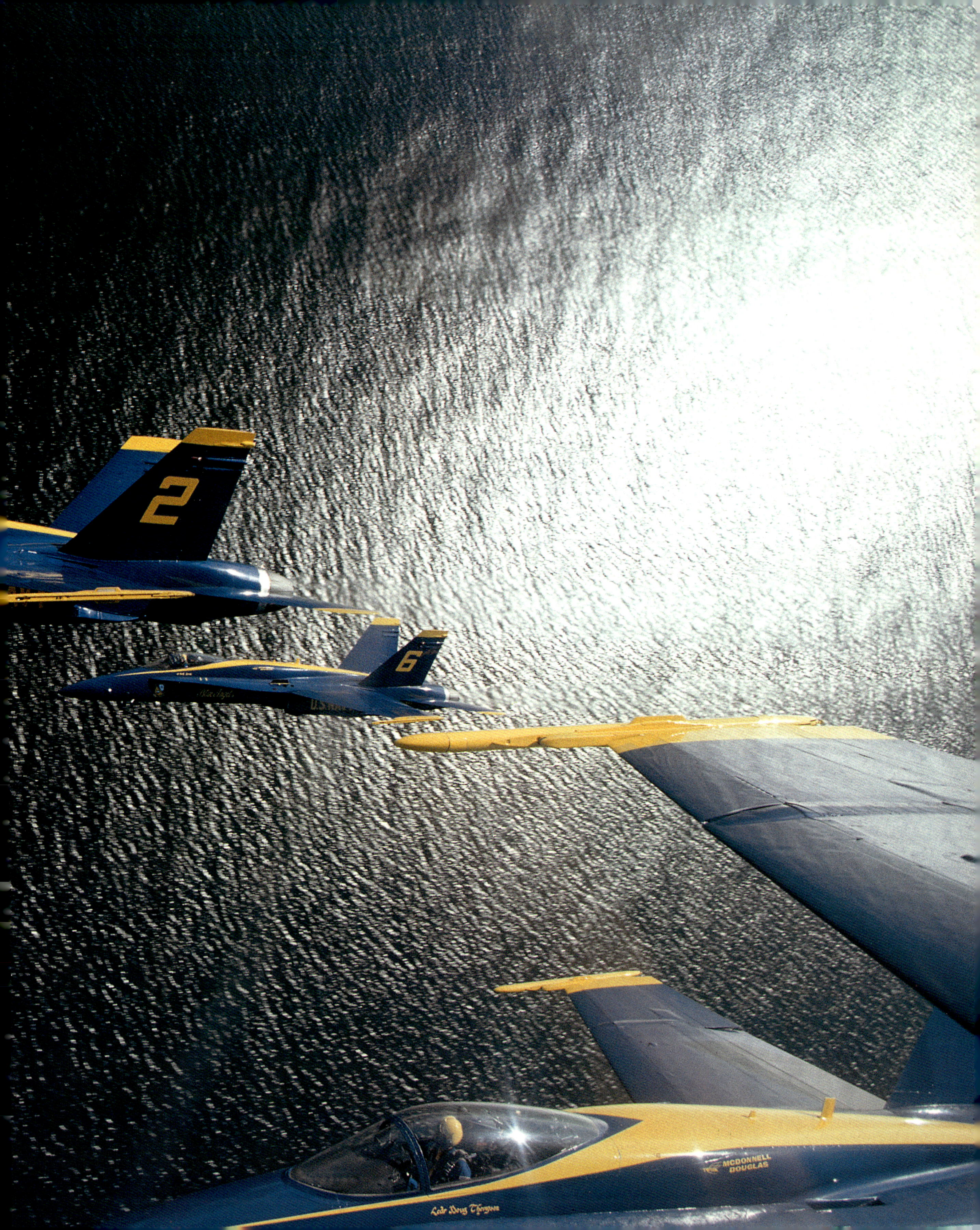
2
6
MCDONNELL
DOUGLAS
Lcdr Doug Thompson

Marine Air.

4 Fat Albert

NAS Pensacola, Florida

✦✦✦✦ In the faint glow of early morning light, the sound of the F/A-18s' twin turbo fans can be heard rumbling through an engine run. Though only Wednesday, Blue Angel #7 is preparing to depart for this weekend's show site at McConnell Air Force Base, Kansas, and maintenance is readying his jet. As the team's Narrator, he will also serve as the "front" man for the squadron, arriving a day ahead of the team to ensure all requirements have been met for the Blues' arrival. Flying the two-seat #7 jet, he brings with him a maintenance specialist to check that all logistical requirements have been met for the parking and servicing of Blue Angel jets. Being ahead of the show schedule is a way of life for #7, and this process began many months ago during the winter training season.

Between December and March, while the six demo pilots were painstakingly learning to fly the show routine, Daddy was already flying to the prospective show sites with #8, the Events Coordinator. Once there, they would meet with the local air show officials and ensure they would be able to meet the team's needs as specified by the Support Manual that had already been forwarded to them. This 80 page document is the bible for any air show committee desiring the Blue Angels, and specifies what the team will need during a typical Thursday through Sunday visit. The manual encompasses jet maintenance requirements, crowd control plans, medial information kits, and airfield specifications. It also includes numerous check lists, which reveal, for example, that the team may use up to fifteen 55 gallon drums of smoke oil for the weekend. The Events Coordinator, Surge, is well versed on all that the manual says – he wrote it.

There are people like Surge in every organization. Working behind the scenes and receiving little recognition for their efforts, they nonetheless are extremely important to the unit's ability to successfully complete its mission. On a team made up of many of these people, Surge is one who wears the blue flight suit, and he is seldom seen except at show center during a performance. #8's assistance to the Narrator during a show is just the most conspicuous of the many responsibilities his position entails.

With two yeomen assigned to his office, he spends much of his time on the phone coordinating a multitude of things, from FAA waivers to team lodging, and he needs to know a little about everyone's job on the team so he can correctly answer inquiries about anything from C-130 JATO bottles to media receptions. His office must stay well ahead of the team's schedule and is normally swamped with paper work and phone calls.

Between the two of them, #7 and #8 ensure that all is smooth for the pilots' arrival at any show site and try to adhere to a regular routine. As Daddy takes off on this Wednesday morning, Surge will stay to brief the pilots on all the particulars about this week's show site. Once at the show site, Daddy will give certain media members a flight in the #7 jet, something Surge has long before coordinated.

✦✦✦✦ As Surge enters the briefing room, the pilots are finishing up their postflight debriefing, but manage to throw a few verbal barbs his way, for no particular reason other than natural reflex. As a Naval Flight Officer, Surge is not intimidated by the pilots, because he has worked closely with their kind in his previous job and is more adept at handling their particular brand of humor than most others on the team.

As a young boy, Surge had seen the Blue Angels perform at the big Reading Air Show in Pennsylvania. From then on, he wanted to fly, and only poor eyesight kept him from becoming a pilot. Ever since that first show, he always had thought the Blue Angels were simply the best flying team in the world. He never thought he would ever be one, but he now plays a key role in their success. He is the first to hear the pilots' discontent when something at a show site is not right (the PAO is a close second), and he is the first to deal with each site's air show committee. Surge is also the first to give full credit for his own success as Events Coordinator to his enlisted staff. He is a man well prepared, and always seems to have a smile for everyone. As he begins to set up for his briefing he simply smiles at the jibes, knowing that no one on the team is immune, and it won't be long before the spotlight shifts.

The shift is already underway. In the aftermath of the morning's debriefing, the Boss is going over a point with Lawman on his rendezvous technique and says, "Instead of closing on my jet as if it's a hard maneuvering target, just view it as a lump of metal with some angle of bank." Timber adds, "Yeah, just like an A-7," referring to the stubby jet the Boss used to fly. With mock indignation, Snooze looks at Dino, both former A-7 jocks, and says, "Did you hear what that solo said?" And with such banter the team winds down from a long debrief session, sits back, and prepares to listen to Surge tell them everything they'll need to know about McConnell and Wichita, Kansas.

Surge goes over the field diagram in great detail, and answers the pilots' many questions as only someone who was well prepared could. The distinct roar of a jet in full afterburner is heard outside, and, as if part of the weekly routine, someone murmurs, "Daddy's off." Thus another air show weekend is put into motion.

As I watched the immense amount of preparation that Daddy and Surge put into each show, I had to wonder just how Butch Voris and his boys in the Bearcats were able to do it all in those early days of Blue Angel performances. But the more I watched these Blues in action, the more evident their teamwork became. Whether they were 36 inches apart in the diamond formation, or thousands of miles away from the squadron at a show site, the Blue Angels truly functioned as a team. Together, the Blues were able to overcome the many difficulties which surfaced weekly.

One of the most visible examples of this team concept, is the Blue Angels' inclusion of their transport aircraft into their show routine. What other team would take their cargo plane, and integrate it into one of the most dynamic performances of the show? This would be a little like race officials at the Indy 500 entering the pace car into the actual race – only much more exciting to watch. (From the very beginning, Blue Angel performances have never lacked showmanship.)

Flown by an all Marine crew, the Blue Angel C-130 Hercules aircraft is affectionately known as Fat Albert. The aircraft is vital to the team as it hauls the necessary men and equipment to the air shows to support those six blue jets. Fat Albert seems to have a distinct personality all its own, and after its menial tasks of transportation are completed, Bert gets right into the air show mode. Used as a show opener for the Blues' performance, Bert is fitted with eight JATO (jet-assisted takeoff) cannisters and performs a short field takeoff maneuver that is always a crowd favorite. When the JATO rockets kick in, Bert's large nose rotates to near 50 degrees of pitch, as the large aircraft nimbly leaps from the runway amidst the deafening roar of eight flame-spewing rockets attached to its fuselage. This is followed by Bert's high speed low altitude pass, from which the four engine turboprop transport enters a max rate climb, all quite impressive from an ungainly looking aircraft that few would associate with high performance. But high performance is exactly what Bert's crew gives the crowd in a memorable demonstration of the Hercules' capabilities in the hands of highly experienced Marine Corps pilots. Capped off with a minimum run landing, and a demonstration of the C-130's unique capability to taxi in reverse, Bert's 15-minute show is complete with the waving of the Stars and Stripes from the top hatch of the plane.

Listening to the crowd's collective verbal response to a Bert performance one day, I thought that it must have been similar to what those early crowds sounded like as they witnessed the "flaming" of a "Japanese Zero" right before their eyes. I never heard anyone call Bert "fat" during its impressive performance.

FAT ALBERT

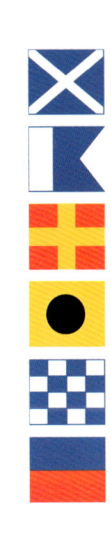

TOP
In the squadron briefing room, Surge gives the pilots a detailed briefing on all the particulars they'll need to know about the week's upcoming show site.

BOTTOM
Wilbur pilots Fat Albert to the next show site. The all-Marine crew of the C-130 has its own office in the squadron and blends in well with the Navy unit it so proudly transports.

74 BLUE ANGELS *A Portrait of Gold*

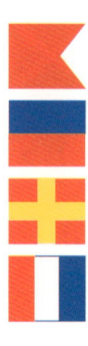

Bert performing the Jet-Assist Takeoff – a true crowd favorite, and an impressive display of the venerable C-130's capabilities.

Unfortunately, not all audiences at Blue Angel demonstrations will get to see Bert perform. The JATO cannisters are an explosive device, and, as such, must be used at airfields only where there are proper storage and handling facilities – normally only military bases.

Like the Narrator and Events Coordinator, the Bert crew is busy during the winter training season, not only hauling supplies from Pensacola to El Centro, California, but also actively partaking in a recruiting role through various trips around the country. While having Marines attached to a Navy squadron is rare, the Blue Angel mix works well, and signifies the productive working relationship between the two services – a concept brought home during C-130 recruiting trips.

Aboard Fat Albert

♦♦♦♦ Climbing aboard Fat Albert on Thursday for transport to McConnell Air Force Base, I become immediately aware of just how small this plane is when matched with the logistical needs of the team. Amidst 25,000 pounds of vital equipment and spare parts, 35 Blue Angel maintenance folks squeeze into the narrow aisle created between the pallets of cargo and Bert's metal body. Touching the shoulders of two maintenance chiefs on either side of me, I sit on a small seat of nylon webbing and aluminum bracing, folded down from the side of the aircraft. The passengers sit facing inward toward the aisle, but can't see anyone on the other side because of the mountain of equipment fastened to the centerline of the very full plane. I've ridden more comfortably when being transported into combat. My view for the next three hours consists of an F/A-18 main landing gear tire, a mere two feet in front of my face.

The noise of Bert's four engines would be overwhelming if it were not for the earplugs that everyone employs. Once airborne, these men, who have learned in their careers to cope with duty on ships, creatively find places to stretch out and sleep. Some read, others work with a laptop computer, and on a tool stand in the back, there is a card game going. Conversations are minimal since shouting is the necessary mode of communication over the din of Bert's engines. Outside on the fuselage of the aircraft, just aft of the Marine Corps emblem, are painted the words "Fat Albert Airlines." As I prop my feet up on the large tire in front of me, and relieve the soundly sleeping chief of his newspaper, the words reflected on Bert's weary body have taken on a whole new meaning.

McConnell Air Force Base, Kansas

♦♦♦♦ People, regardless of their level of understanding of jet formation flying, all seem genuinely excited about the Blue Angels coming to their city. The team almost never stays on base for military shows, seeking instead a downtown hotel removed from the crowds and traffic of an air show weekend. At each hotel, the staff seems to enjoy serving as hosts to this well known team. In each Blue Angel's room in Wichita, there was a plate of cookies, cut in the shape of little Hornet jets and coated with blue icing.

Briefing

♦♦♦♦ McConnell is hotter than Phoenix today, hitting temperatures of 120 degrees on the flightline. Prior to the briefing, the pilots eat lunch, along with Cubby, Mo, and the C-130 pilots. These people burn a lot of calories in a day and there seem to be no vegetarians in the group as a stack of sub sandwiches is devoured.

Earlier this morning, most of them were lifting weights at a local athletic club, part of their daily routine while on the road. When Daddy and Surge were setting up team accommodations months ago, one of the prerequisites was to locate and obtain guest passes for a nearby workout facility.

Staying in shape is critical for this type of flying. The weight lifting improves one's G tolerance, and in a show where jets will fluctuate between -2.0G to +7.5G, the pilots better have that tolerance. Another requirement for Blue Angel pilots is building the right arm strength, since the team's F/A-18s are rigged differently than the regular fleet Hornets. To keep a positive (pulling) feel on the stick at all times, throughout a wide speed range,

Blue Angel jets have been modified with a spring tension device on the stick in each cockpit. This tension allows the pilots to keep a continuous pressure on the stick, or relax that pressure, as necessary in the formation. Without it, there would at times be some slight pushing forward on the stick to maintain one's position, and that would cause the kind of dangerous pitch movements unacceptable in a formation this tight. With this "heavy" stick feel of 30-35 pounds of pressure, Blue Angel pilots fly the formation by resting their forearm across their leg, and use mostly wrist action to make the minutely precise movements on the stick that such close flying requires. They have been doing it this way for many years, and is that why the team never wore G-suits. Encircling both legs, the G-suit would constantly be inflating and deflating with the various G loads, moving the forearm resting on the right leg, thus disrupting the very subtle wrist movements occurring continously in order for the pilot to remain in proper position. Between the heavy pressure that must be held against the stick just to hold level flight, and the immense G loads the body suffers without a G-suit during a Blues' routine, physical fitness is not simply recommended – it is a requirement. Building up their right arms, pilots develop what they call the "lobster arm." When you shake hands with these people, it can hurt.

✦✦✦✦ While finishing lunch, Hoops tosses a joking remark toward one of the C-130 pilots. The Marine quickly replies, "You know, your luggage doesn't have to make it back to Pensacola." Snooze quickly points out that he was not the one who made the remark, nor would he ever make such a remark to the crew that carries his luggage.

✦✦✦✦ I will fly with Snooze today for a practice show for the base. This is uncommon as hardly anyone ever gets to fly with Blue Angel #3; normally, he would be in his first year, and the team tries not to burden new guys with guest flyers. #3 normally moves to the slot in his second year, but this year Dino was kept an extra season for continuity, so Snooze comfortably sits on the wing for a second year as #3. This affords me a rare opportunity to see, from the one position with the least clearance from the Boss' jet, the maneuver that defines the Blue Angel diamond as the world's tightest formation.

The Diamond 360, flown early in the show sequence, is probably the most photographed of all Blue Angel formations, and is their tightest. In essence, the maneuver is a simple level arc in front of the crowd, but there is nothing simple about putting four jets together that close in flight. In order to make it look symmetrical to the crowd at show center, each wingman is actually flying slightly offset, each in a little different position from normal. For #3, who is on the inside of the turn, this means putting his canopy directly beneath the Boss' left wing, with the narrowest of clearance. I am anxious to see what the world's tightest formation looks like from this closest of perspectives.

Snooze and I have flown together before, but weather dictated it be a low show, and I'm glad today's weather is better. We talk about the A-7, a plane we both used to fly, and the many improvements that the newer F/A-18 offers. Snooze is easy to talk with, and seems as relaxed as someone who is preparing to simply take the car out for a drive. Part of his calm demeanor comes from his being in his second year with the team, but mostly, it's due to Snooze's personality.

Each of the six men sitting around the table brings his own particular personality to the team, and they must all blend in the interest of team unity. Watching this blend as these men interact at work and play, I observe that each member seems to have their own particular personality "role" that helps keep the team balanced.

The Boss most often displays a stoic calm, even in the face of severe turmoil, thus helping keep the team focused and less distracted. Solo pilot Hoops can be intimidating, with his 6'3" body chiseled from the heavy steel of weight rooms. He doesn't say too much, but when he does, his words are direct and to the point – unyielding and accurate. And that's just the way the team wants the lead solo to be. Everything about Hoops' demeanor securely conveys to the team that the solos will be precisely where they are supposed to be, when they are supposed to be there – even if it hurts, which most of their routine does. People seem to kid Hoops the least. And of course there is Dino, able to police the diamond with a stern tone when necessary, and the experience to know when to use it.

Although other members of the team contribute roles too, Snooze's personality fulfills one that is vital to the team's mental health. Snooze is like the good little schoolboy who the teacher is always surprised to discover was involved in some prank. And due to his infectious grin, he often gets away with it. Snooze, now over the difficulties of learning his position, seems able to provide the team with doses of relaxed humor from time to time. Unlike the pointed humor the team most often directs toward each other, this is more generic and affords everyone a good laugh. More than just a conscious effort, this role seems to come naturally from this former collegiate baseball player. He loves to tell stories, and will feign innocence when one of his pranks is uncovered. It is Snooze's sense of timing, however, that is so important in keeping an even balance to the team's mood. After a long harangue by Dino, Snooze knows when to add a touch of levity, and more importantly, when not to. Though he realizes just exactly what Lawman is going through in his first year, Snooze is the first to kid him about being a Marine. Many days that is the best feeling of "belonging" that Lawman will experience.

After a particularly bad day when no one felt good about his performance, there was an obvious absence of the usual sarcastic humor. There was Snooze, jumping in to explain why his smoke came on at the wrong time with an innovative story about his large watch bumping the smoke switch on the throttle. This rivaled even his previous story about a bee in the cockpit. The effect on the team was similar to throwing a magnet into a box of metal filings, and the comments from the others flew. Satisfied that the team was back on track, Snooze, with that schoolboy grin, claimed, "That's my story and I'm sticking to it."

Snooze's particular brand of humor is fed to the team in small dosages, strategically given out when they are most needed. Not far removed is the very serious and intense side of Snooze, though, and for all his enthusiastic laughter, few would characterize him as carefree and easy going. Like the others, he is very serious about his flying – and is very good at it.

No one doubts his ability to handle all that he'll inherit with the #4 position next season. He relishes being part of the diamond. Like previous Blues, Snooze admits that Blue Angel flying is more difficult than anticipated: "That first winter training is a bear, and battling the frustration of not getting it down right away can really eat at you. It's like chopping a tree down, but you can't use an ax, just a pocket knife, and you must whittle away at it a little at a time to get those maneuvers down. I thought I understood concentration before I came here – I didn't. I do now."

Flight with #3

✦✦✦✦ As we taxi out, Snooze talks with me, between necessary radio calls, and sounds as calm as if we were still sitting in the briefing room, instead of approaching the runway for a diamond takeoff. In less than a minute after takeoff, we are going to be on our back, completing the top of the diamond loop. This is not something you warm up to, you simply come prepared. I look over at Dino, taxiing a couple of feet off our wing. He and Snooze have known each other since their A-7 days, and frequently exchange private hand signals. It helps keep them loose.

The Diamond 360 is the second maneuver in the diamond's sequence, so there is hardly time to work up to flying the tightest formation of the day. Immediately after takeoff, we enter the loop and Snooze has ceased talking. The only sound on the radio is the calm voice of the Boss, cueing the others when he is about to pull into the vertical. The most intriguing sound, though, is the tempest fury created by the other six afterburners next to us.

The diamond loop completed, the solo pilots now execute their takeoff maneuvers, as we fly behind the crowd and begin the arc which will eventually see us perform nearly 360 degrees of turn. Snooze begins to settle the jet into the slightly offset position he will hold throughout the maneuver. I ready my camera and plan to get a shot of the Boss' wing once we are tucked in beneath it.

Within moments, we are in position and approaching the crowd. There is no picture I can take. As we approach the runway, I take the camera from my eye and simply hold it in my lap. We are so close to the Boss' wing that I would need an even wider lens than I have to show anything other than just a mass of blue. I see the Boss' yellow missile rail so close to my helmet that if there were no canopy, I could reach out and touch it. I instinctively lower my seat a notch, realizing for the first time that, if we bump, it's my head that will be hit first. I want to look at Dino, tucked snugly into the slot now, but I can't bring myself to look away from the little screws that I notice for the first time on the flap hinge of Boss' jet.

Snooze, in that calm tone of voice that tells me he is seriously concentrating, says "This is when you really learn what trusting your Leader is all about." He is so right. One miscue from Boss now, one bird strike, any oscillation, and we would simply collide. There is a great deal of trust here, and I am gaining a bunch of it in a hurry. The air is smooth, and for just a moment, Snooze squeezes it in even tighter, I think just to impress the Air Force guy sitting in his back seat. He did. I have flown tight before, and even scared myself. I have never flown that tight before on purpose.

As we pass the crowd line and ease it out a bit to set up for the diamond roll, Snooze remarks with the relieved voice of someone who has trespassed across a forbidden line and gotten away with it, "That'll give you religion!" Snooze will cross that line every time the team flies, as a matter of routine – concentrated routine.

Boss tells the formation to "ease it out," and they loosen their formation a bit as they position for the next maneuver. Watching the Boss' jet, I can see the automatic leading edge flap on his wing continue to position itself based on his angle of attack and airspeed. A smaller flap surface on the trailing edge of the F/A-18's wing does the same thing, causing it to be known as the "living wing" among Hornet pilots. This technology gives the F/A-18 superb maneuverability and increases greatly the margin of safety for pilots prone to fly the plane to its limits. These guys do.

As we move into echelon formation, Lawman sets the rate of movement for the rest of the formation. Once we are tucked snugly up near #2, Snooze can listen to the engines of the two planes close in front of him for cues in power changes. If Lawman bobbles here, Snooze has to refrain from the reflex of countering it too quickly, as Dino is now snugly flying up against our fuselage. When 16 tons of airplane get in your face, this is easier said than done.

Flying in echelon this close is difficult enough, but, as with most of their performance, the Blues challenge themselves with taking the formation where few would go. They are the only team that perform a rolling maneuver into the echelon, a maneuver not recommended in all basic formation guides. Once into the maneuver, there is little doubt why it is not recommended. Strung out, laterally offset, on a line, the formation has to somehow adjust as Boss rolls into them, and they curl beneath the roll axis.

Up close, the maneuver looks every bit as difficult and dangerous as its reputation, and Snooze begins to talk in the front seat. Snooze will frequently talk to himself while flying. Sometimes it is directed towards himself, many times towards the others. Today he is offering some succinct assessments of Lawman's movements. Scattered between these short, tension-filled exclamations are apologies thrown Dino's way, as Snooze realizes Dino is bearing the brunt of everyone's movements. As if the planes were puppets, all held together with the same string, they bob and weave through the dictations of a maneuver that one never perfects, but merely survives. Once over, Snooze completes his assessment with a final "We're gonna hear about *that* one later," and seems genuinely pleased to move on to the next maneuver.

Flightline McConnell

✦✦✦✦ It remains hot for the big show day, but the clouds break enough for a high show. Fat Albert dazzles a crowd that is used to seeing large multi-engine planes fly out of McConnell, but not like this. Kids in the crowd are quick to pick up certain nuances about the team that adults sometimes miss, although they aren't always as precise. As Bert taxied in, one little girl pointed out, "There goes Fat Wilbur."

As Daddy narrates the main performance facing the crowd, Surge watches the movements of the planes to help cue the narration. Daddy will spend one season as Narrator, and then move to either a wing or solo position the next two years. Being the #7 pilot has its advantages, but the drawbacks are having to leave a day early to get to each show, and then having to depart each show site ahead of the team to check the next one. When the Narrator is most in step with the team, though, is during the performance when his words are timed exactly to describe the flying overhead.

Shortly into the show, Snooze has a problem with his jet and is forced to land. The ground crew already has the #7 jet running. Snooze climbs down from his plane and into the spare with little delay. Meanwhile, Dino has moved into the #3 position, and the show continues with the little "V" formation instead of the diamond. Within minutes, Snooze is taxiing to join the formation overhead.

This is a tricky rendezvous, as the Boss is not going to alter the pattern or timing of any of the maneuvers to facilitate the rejoin. Snooze must simply time it so that he can rejoin the formation in time for them to be set for the next maneuver. He must know exactly where the other five jets are so as not to conflict with any of them on his way back to the Boss' left wing.

As Snooze taxies the two-seater past Surge and Daddy on his way to the runway, a young boy in the front of the crowd yells to Daddy. Having witnessed Snooze's quick commandeering of the #7 jet, and getting no response from Daddy, the boy persists. Finally he is heard to say, quite emphatically, "Hey #7, someone is taking your jet!" Luckily, there was a break in the narration at that point in the show, and Daddy put the microphone down for a moment. He and Surge just smiled at each other. Daddy's narrations were always most professional, and I never heard him deviate from the script – except this once. Noting the honest concern in the young boy's repeated voice, Daddy yelled back, off mic, "It's OK, I said he could borrow it." And Snooze rejoined smoothly, and the show went on; and at least one young boy on a hot, sunny day in Kansas was satisfied that all was in order.

80 | BLUE ANGELS *A Portrait of Gold*

The pilots enter their jets separately as they perform the march-down at the beginning of the show; but on landing, the team waits for Boss' signal to exit their jets in unison.

FAT ALBERT

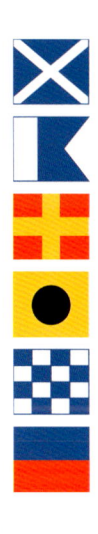

Crew chiefs hustle to clear jets prior to engine start. After the show, they will push each plane back into a straight parking line for the next day's performance.

82 BLUE ANGELS *A Portrait of Gold*

TOP
Dino and Snooze wait for Bert to complete its show before lining up for the march-down. Flying pals from previous days, these two pilots represent five years of Blue Angel experience.

BOTTOM
Surge watches the jets taxi out as Daddy narrates the action.

FAT ALBERT

*The slot man.
The grin.*

OVERLEAF
*The Diamond 360
as seen from
the #3 position.
From this distance,
Snooze can see his
own reflection in the
Boss' wing.*

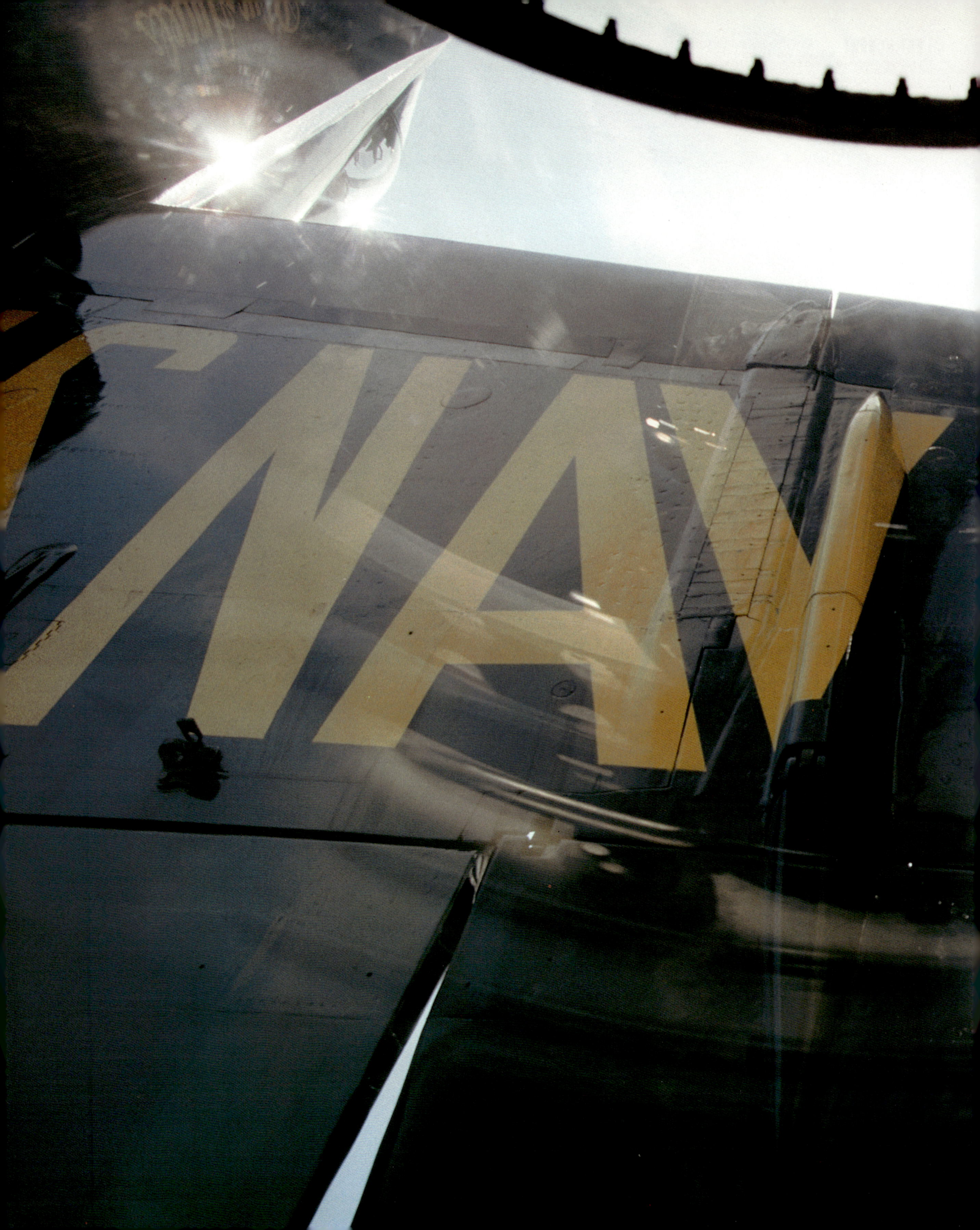

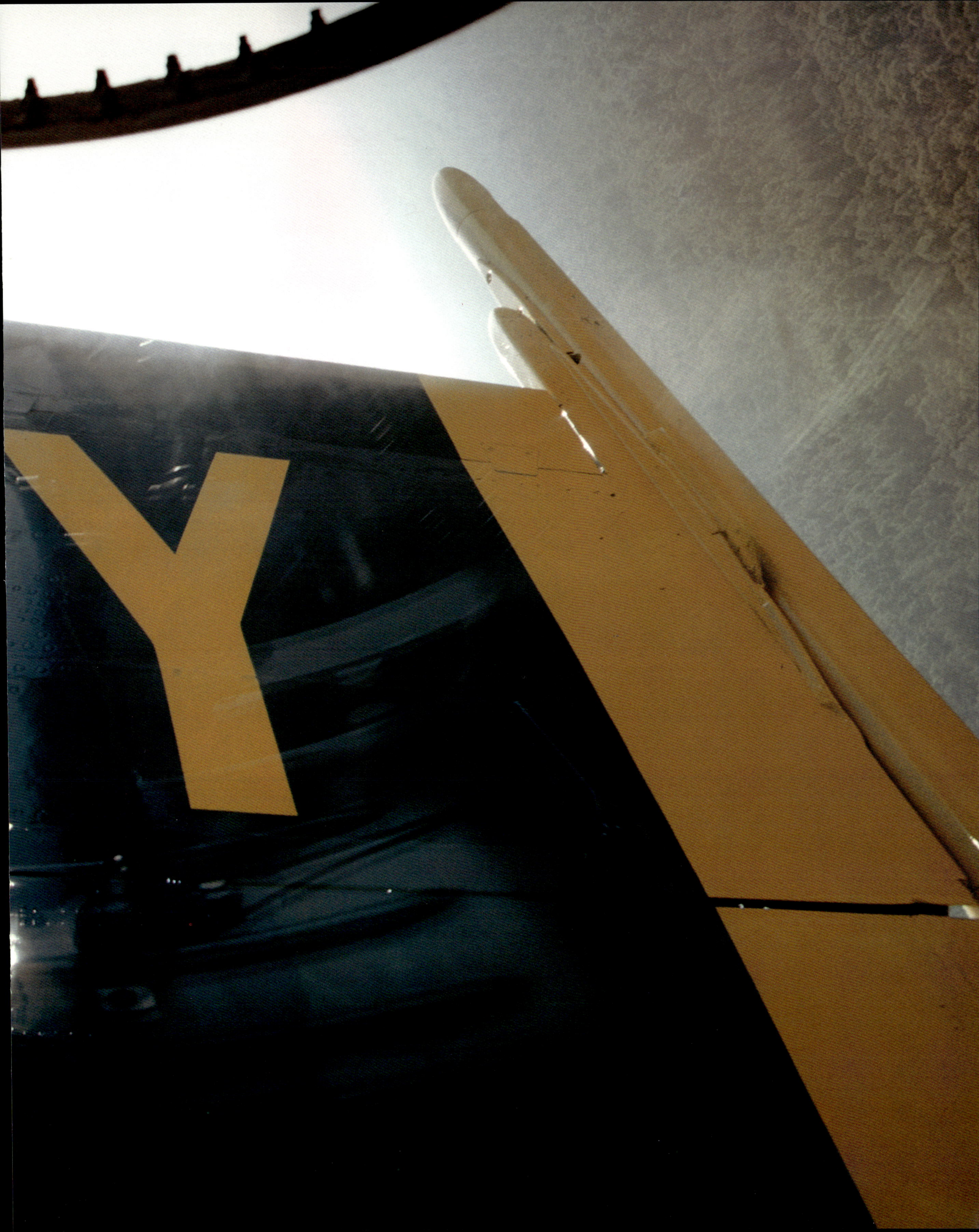

BLUE ANGELS *A Portrait of Gold*

5 Feet Wet

Traverse City, Michigan

♦♦♦♦ The amount of work and effort that goes into each show is impressive. There is hardly time to eat, and I now understand why team members grab a snack whenever they can. The days can be very long, and they aren't over until everything gets done.

Bert began loading this morning at 0430 at Pensacola. By 0630, it was crammed with men and material and on its way to Traverse City. Arriving before the jets, crews spent the early morning at Traverse unloading equipment, positioning equipment for the jets' arrival, securing the rental cars, setting up the briefing room, and preparing for the media interviews.

The blue jets arrive around midday after two hops. Approaching the field, the diamond breaks up into a loose formation and spends the next 15 minutes surveying the local area for key geographic reference points that they have only previously viewed on their maps. They also take note of such hazards as high towers and sharply rising terrain. Both are present at this location. These "arrival maneuvers" are accomplished at each show site and are as important for the wingmen as the Boss, since several Blue Angel maneuvers involve the splitting of the formation and the use of individual reference points by everyone.

Meanwhile, the solo jets have landed and are being refueled, and Cubby has already set up Hoops for an interview with a local TV station. When the diamond lands, they proceed to debrief in a room, complete with the necessary video equipment, that has already been set up by early arriving team members.

Then the solos take to the air and perform a similar check of the area as did the diamond, but in more detail. The solos actually fly through several of their maneuvers to check their critical timing and reference points. Once down, they will join the rest of the team in the debriefing room.

Once the pilots are all together, Daddy briefs them on the particulars of rental cars, lodging, directions to the hotel and athletic club, and any other details that might ease their transition from the confines of a sweaty cockpit to a hot shower. Many sandwiches are devoured. Everyone looks beat. The team agrees that a practice with everyone would be a good idea, since the show area is over Lake Michigan and water shows are always a little different. The team briefs and flies, and for the solo pilots, it is their fourth flight of the day.

While the team is flying, I watch the Bert crew work to remove an engine which had to be shut down en route. Neat clumps of C-130 parts are all over the hangar floor, but arrangements have already been made to have another engine flown in late tonight. Some people will have an early wake-up tomorrow. I watch Cubby, still patiently answering questions from certain media folks who showed up two hours late and didn't enter the area at the proper gate, thus causing a security problem. They want to know why the pilots aren't there ready for them – and, by the way, can one of our guys get a flight with the team? Cubby's patience is phenomenal, but at this point in the day, he has that look that tells me those folks are close to their last questions, even if they don't know it. I see several maintenance specialists crowded around the #7 jet trying to solve an elusive electrical problem that has plagued the plane for a week now. Mo and Doc have driven out to the edge of the lake to monitor the practice, along with the video cameraman.

When the practice is over and the long debrief is completed, a weary team finally heads to the hotel.

Everyone has been busy since 0400 this morning, and after some long flights, much setting up, a couple of emergencies, media interviews, and a prolonged day of maintenance, they check into their rooms at 1930.

There is a recurring belief around the air show circuit that holds how glamorous life must be as a Blue Angel on tour. Perhaps it could be. As a quiet group of mechanics sat on the hangar floor that evening, sorting and tagging every C-130 part, there were no cheering crowds.

Traverse City

♦♦♦♦ This is the heart of the summer air show season now, and the Traverse City Cherry Festival in July represents that atmosphere wonderfully. Even the weather cooperates, and one could find few settings as enjoyable as this small resort community in which to enjoy the Blue Angels' performance. With thousands of summer tourists crowding the lakefront park to watch the performance, the show is flown mainly over the water, and the team launches and recovers from the nearby Coast Guard base.

Overwater shows present certain unique challenges to the team. Often, air currents will change radically between the water and the surrounding coastal terrain. This was a prominent occurrence at Traverse, as strong winds from northern Lake Michigan hit the rolling hills of the Traverse cove. During the performance, the jets transition from land to water throughout their maneuvering, thus causing some plowing through unseen waves of turbulence with each entry and exit. The Traverse performances were as bumpy to fly as they were beautiful to watch.

Briefing

♦♦♦♦ Deep into the season now, the team is starting to come together in performance, as well as in personality. As they gather in the briefing room prior to the Friday practice show, I notice that even Lawman is starting to smile a little more often. Most on the team agree that it takes about six months for the group to really get comfortable in their formation.

During the usual feasting on snacks that occurs prior to the briefing, Snooze, for no particular reason, launches into recounting hilarious stories about experiences he had while living aboard carriers at sea. There is no shortage of enthusiasm as he speaks, and it's contagious. The Boss, who by the very nature of his position rarely gets to unwind fully, joins in with some even funnier stories about life aboard "the boat," and recounts them with a verve and humor that is refreshing to see from one who carries the weight of the team on his shoulders. Soon everyone is recounting his own hellish or humorous story about life on the "boat" – from bad catapult launches to suffering a water stoppage in the shower after being fully soaped. These are anecdotes that only Navy aviators who have lived and flown on carriers could tell, and they are told with a gusto that reveals some amount of relief to now be on firm ground at Traverse City. For a few moments amidst resounding laughter, six men who have experienced much in their young lives are able to set aside the air show they are about to fly and relive former days of daring. In the process of strengthening the bond of their common experience, they now know each other a little better.

Listening to their assortment of tales, I find it amazing that they are alive today at all. I can discern from their words, though, that aside from their special blue flight suits, they are really no different than all those Navy flyers still out there, whom they now represent. More than once I've heard the pilots tell me this year that they aren't any different from their pals back in the fleet; they just have practiced the routine more. Lots more. The theme of "just regular guys, working hard" continues to surface with this team as I continue to get to know them better. The pilots seem to prefer this image to all others, and I sense it may be the most accurate.

These moments prior to every briefing are preciously guarded by the team from outsiders, and in their way serve to help weave a cohesive thread that binds six different lives tightly together for a year. It is a time for them to relax, and steal some common moments from the pressures of their very uncommon job.

FEET WET

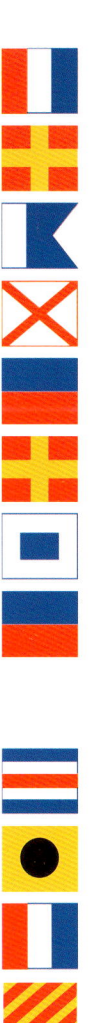

BLUE ANGELS *A Portrait of Gold*

As the laughter subsides, the Boss glances at his watch, and with a quiet "OK, let's begin," brings the team soberly back to the present task at hand of briefing to put six jets, safely and precisely, through 28 of the most challenging maneuvers they'll ever fly. In stark contrast to the exuberant laughter just witnessed, the quiet intensity of their faces now gives pause to wonder if their shipboard trials will truly define all that was difficult and intimidating in their Navy careers – or if this will.

Debriefing

♦♦♦♦ Listening to the debriefing, one would think the team flew pretty poorly, but in fact they had a good day today overall. Dino needs to drive home some hard points, though, and does, but wisely follows his most pointed remarks with sly humor. He is careful not to destroy the positive feeling the team had today about their flying, and wants them to build on that for the big shows in the next two days. Dino is as much psychologist as instructor, and there is always a delicate balance in being able to tell such talented individuals just how poorly they executed a maneuver. What makes #4's job easier, though, is that these people usually know exactly what they did wrong, agree with the assessment, and make a mental note to correct it next time. There is never a perfect performance. I only heard the word "good" used twice all summer. Aside from being the world's biggest kidders, this is a team of serious professional aviators, each one driven toward excellence. They do not tolerate repeated mistakes well.

Boss is having some inconsistencies with his roll rate. This affects the wingmen dramatically in their ability to match the lead aircraft throughout the maneuver. Often, when the solos, who make up the end points of the six-plane Delta formation, fall slightly out of position, the reason may be linked to the Boss' roll technique. The Boss must be consistent, every day, in everything he does in the air. "Smooth" must become a way of life for him. One errant move of throttles in the Line-Abreast Loop, and the four planes next to him will all look out of position. The Boss not only holds the key to the success of each maneuver in his hands, he also holds – as firmly as his grip on the stick – the very lives of those flying next to him.

Not everyone wants to be the Leader of the Blue Angels. Not everyone can. The Boss is only the 24th man in Blue Angel history to hold the position, and like the rest, he never thought he'd be out in front of the Navy's most recognized unit when he first started flying. That the Boss would start flying at all was somewhat in doubt during his early naval training.

The Boss, whose father and grandfather were career Army officers, attended school at Annapolis and was considering a career in nuclear submarines until the summer of his junior year. While on an orientation cruise, he met a Navy pilot, became friends, and was impressed with the flier's upbeat attitude. When he saw the same aviator, weeks later, make a low fly-by across the bow of the ship, he knew something other than the serious, silent life of the submariner was calling him.

Excelling as a fighter pilot, the Boss was part of the Navy's first F/A-18 squadron. In spite of his impressive naval flying career, which includes over 900 carrier landings, he emphatically states that being Blue Angel Leader is "the hardest thing I've ever done." This stems from the superhuman requirement levied on the Leader of the Blues to provide a consistently stable platform for the wingmen to fly off of, every time, in every maneuver.

Few men in the Navy are more at home in the Hornet than Boss, but after the debrief, he admits that he's more accustomed to success than failure, and confesses, "It bugs the hell out of me when I know I am not doing it exactly right. In anything else, you'd identify the problem, correct it, and then move on. Normally with enough time and effort into something you can master it, but you can't with this; the dynamics of four planes together make the formation different every time you fly and it challenges you every day, and humbles you every day."

The Boss' frustration is only slightly lessened with the knowledge that it has always been this way since Commander Voris led the first show, and on occasion, rolled inconsistently, causing his wingmen to roll out precariously close to that big propeller up front. But the Boss' desire to do it exactly right is simply the striving for uncompromising perfection that enables these men to do what some would consider the impossible.

Though the Boss is not actually flying off of anyone else's airplane, the dynamics of the tight diamond formation are such that when stacked in too closely, the wingmen can actually "lead" the Boss' jet somewhat, with the flow of aerodynamic disturbances between the aircraft. The Boss will feel a pronounced push from underneath his jet if the boys are getting too tight, and this can be quite disconcerting to the one man tasked with flying the most precise and safe course for the others. Once, while leading the Echelon Parade pass, Boss felt the insidious push, and found himself low, pointed 10 degrees pitch down at the end of the maneuver. This was not a comfortable situation in a formation where the smallest oscillation from any of its members can cause disaster.

Regardless of his stature on the team, the Boss takes his "hits" in the debriefings as much as anyone. So strong is the team's cohesion that whatever pressure the Boss feels to perform well comes not from the crowd or the US Navy, but from simply the strong desire to be a good Leader to his wingmen. He feels best when he knows he's made their job a little easier.

With Dino tucked squarely under Boss' 'burner cans in the slot, there is little the Boss can do that will go unnoticed. But the Boss, like the others, takes it in stride as simply a part of the team process and readily states, "We must be brutally honest with each other, and sometimes there is some biting of the lip, but we all have to just leave it at the debriefing table." They do this better than any other group of accomplished, strong willed individuals I have ever seen, and their Leader sets the example, sometimes evoking that serious, quiet demeanor suggestive of the submarine commander he might have been.

Watching the Boss throughout the summer, and seeing all the joy he helped bring to thousands of people, I always felt like he should be allowed to enjoy himself more than he was. In time, I realized, though, that he had his own effective and quiet way of dealing with all that his position demands, and was definitely a man whose priorities were in order.

Although leading the Blue Angels may be the most difficult thing he has done, it is not the most important, as that position is reserved for his family. Occasionally, Boss' wife has taken the opportunity to join her husband at a show site and enjoys watching the Blue Angels perform as much as any spectator in the crowd. Along with three lovely daughters at home, she helps form the Boss' one perfect diamond.

Athletic Club

Though the team operates cohesively, members don't always hang out with each other in their spare time. Just as each member of the formation has a space which cannot be violated, so too, the pilots give each other space during off hours and are not always together. One activity, however, that often does put them together in their free time is their gym workouts.

♣♣♣♣ Cubby calls my room at 0730 to inform me that only pregnant women and Air Force pilots will probably want to miss the workout, but the real men are heading for the gym in thirty minutes. I think Cubby is starting to like me.

Physical fitness has been a way of life for many of these guys long before they came to the team, and once they wrestled the bear called Winter Training Season, they were glad it was. Except for Cubby and Lawman, who are equally shorter than the rest, this is not a small group of men. When they go to the gym, they toss some serious iron. Even Lawman at 5'8", and 160 pounds, can bench press 275, and can hurt your hand with his grip. He's a Marine.

Other members of the team work out also, but rarely come to the gym with the pilots. Mo can be seen jogging most mornings, and the Fat Albert crew normally gets in a run in the evening.

Cubby is the rare exception, the non-pilot who is invited to come along to the gym with the flyers. Though the pilots kid the PAO about being at the "bottom of the food chain," the meat-eaters have allowed him to lift with them. On a team where performance is used to measure respect, the pilots are less concerned with rank or wings and are more impressed with how well someone performs their specialty, and as such, have a strong respect for Cubby as squadron PAO.

The PAO on this team can do much to make life easier for the pilots. They know that Cubby staunchly defends them from the onslaught of thrill seekers and undisciplined media, and helps protect the little privacy they do enjoy. They, of course, cannot say this directly to Cubby in so many words; however, they willingly accepted him into the group when he showed a sincere interest in working out with them. In actuality, these men would welcome anyone on the team who wanted to work out with them. Cubby was just the one who asked, and has earned their respect with the way he has applied himself. This, of course, has had no impact whatsoever in the lessening of "shots" fired at Cubby throughout the process, but it has enabled him to occasionally fire some back.

Under the tutelage of Hoops, Cubby has made great strides in developing his body. But more importantly, through this time spent with the team, he has come to better understand this entity called "fighter pilot" that for Cubby, like many naval officers, has been something of an enigma. Cubby is proud of his acceptance into this inner circle of "the guys," and no one works harder in the weight room – except Hoops.

Snooze, no slouch himself, watches Hoops and Timber lift and says, "Those guys are animals. They enjoy hurting their bodies; that's why they're the solos."

Hoops tells an eager Cubby, "Today we're working back and legs." The workouts are not a competition, but rather a team exercise in conditioning, and shouts of encouragement are frequent. Constantly pulling against the "heavy" stick forces in their jets, and sustaining the punishment of excessive G forces without a G-suit, these men have made the weight room an integral part of their regimen.

✦✦✦✦ As the team enters the gym in Traverse City, no one really pays any attention, since they are dressed in an assortment of regular workout attire, nothing denoting their association with the Blue Angels. Ironically, Snooze is wearing his California Angels baseball shirt, with the logo ANGELS emblazoned across his chest.

The club is small, but not too crowded, and the team really likes it because there is a good selection of free weights. Snooze and Lawman ask some of the local boys if they can work in on the bench with them. The young men treat Snooze and Lawman as if they were regulars at the club, having no idea that they are lifting weights with the two wingmen of the famed Blue Angel diamond. The team likes it this way, just blending in somewhat incognito. The locals were impressed, though, when the unimposing figure of Lawman lifted that big barbell with ease. As a small number of local patrons randomly watch these men flex, sweat, and push heavy metal in an obscure little weight room in Traverse City, little do they know that in a few short hours, this band of brothers will be flexing, sweating, and pushing even more impressive blue metal through the sky in front of a very large audience, riveted to their every move.

Cubby looks at me, stares at my weights, and reprimands, "Are you going to put some weight on that thing, or are you just going to embarrass us all?" When Cubby runs with the wolves, his teeth get sharpened. I think I like this group.

94   BLUE ANGELS *A Portrait of Gold*

TOP
When taking off from a remote site, the show opener consists of the team flying into the performance area in the Delta formation, and having the solos break off.

BOTTOM
The Line-Abreast Loop – a tough one to line up consistently.

FEET WET

Left to right, top to bottom:

BOSS
LAWMAN
SNOOZE
DINO
HOOPS
TIMBER

In the briefing room, the pilots became very predictable in their behavior prior to each show. Each man had his own way to relax and prepare for the performance. No one ever mentioned fear of a mishap, but always in the back of their minds was the deadly serious realization that men had died doing this. These private thoughts, and any apprehensions they had, were handled in a variety of ways, and the pilots' pre-show behavior became as consistent as their formation flying.
The Boss was quietly serious, intent on getting every detail down right.
Lawman silently reviewed airfield data repeatedly, testing himself to not make any repeated mistakes from one show to the next.
Snooze could tell stories that would make everyone relax, and the bigger the show, the more involved his story.
Dino was detached, much like a ball player before an important game who knew what was expected of him, and could swing his mood from laughter to serious comtemplation, finding a middle ground that prevented him from becoming too intense.
Hoops was intense, but the intensity so fit his personality that to be any other way would have seemed abnormal.
Reviewing the solos maneuvers with Timber, he went over every detail, every radio call, every nuance to each new location; and as he did Timber mentally flew the show in his mind, as if in prayer-like meditation. These men never left the room unprepared for the show; and they never had a mishap.

BLUE ANGELS *A Portrait of Gold*

The Pensacola Beach show is a big one every summer, and thousands of tourists line the beaches and clog the main thoroughfares in anticipation of watching the Blue Angels perform. While waiting, this man molded Blue Angel solos in the Fortus maneuver out of beach sand and food dye, in hopes of making the local paper. He didn't; but he did make the book.

FEET WET

The Double Farvel
as seen from
Dino's plane.
Moving slightly aft,
he calls clear of the
Boss, and they both
roll inverted.
Once the Boss is set,
Dino then drives
into position.
The small boat just
under Boss' wing
signifies show center.

OVERLEAF

The Diamond 360
as seen from the slot.
This is the tightest
formation of the day.
It may be the tightest
flown anywhere.

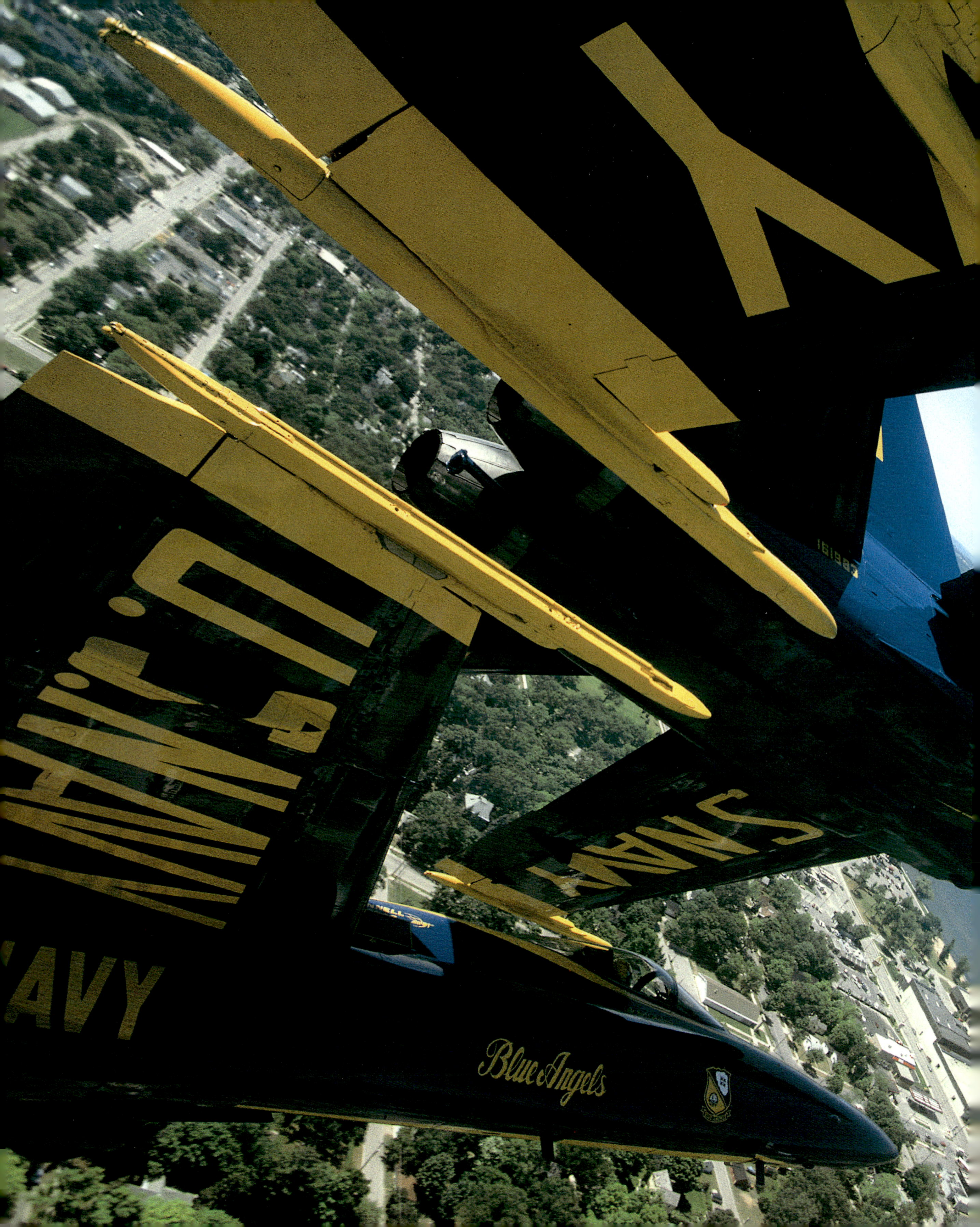
Blue Angels

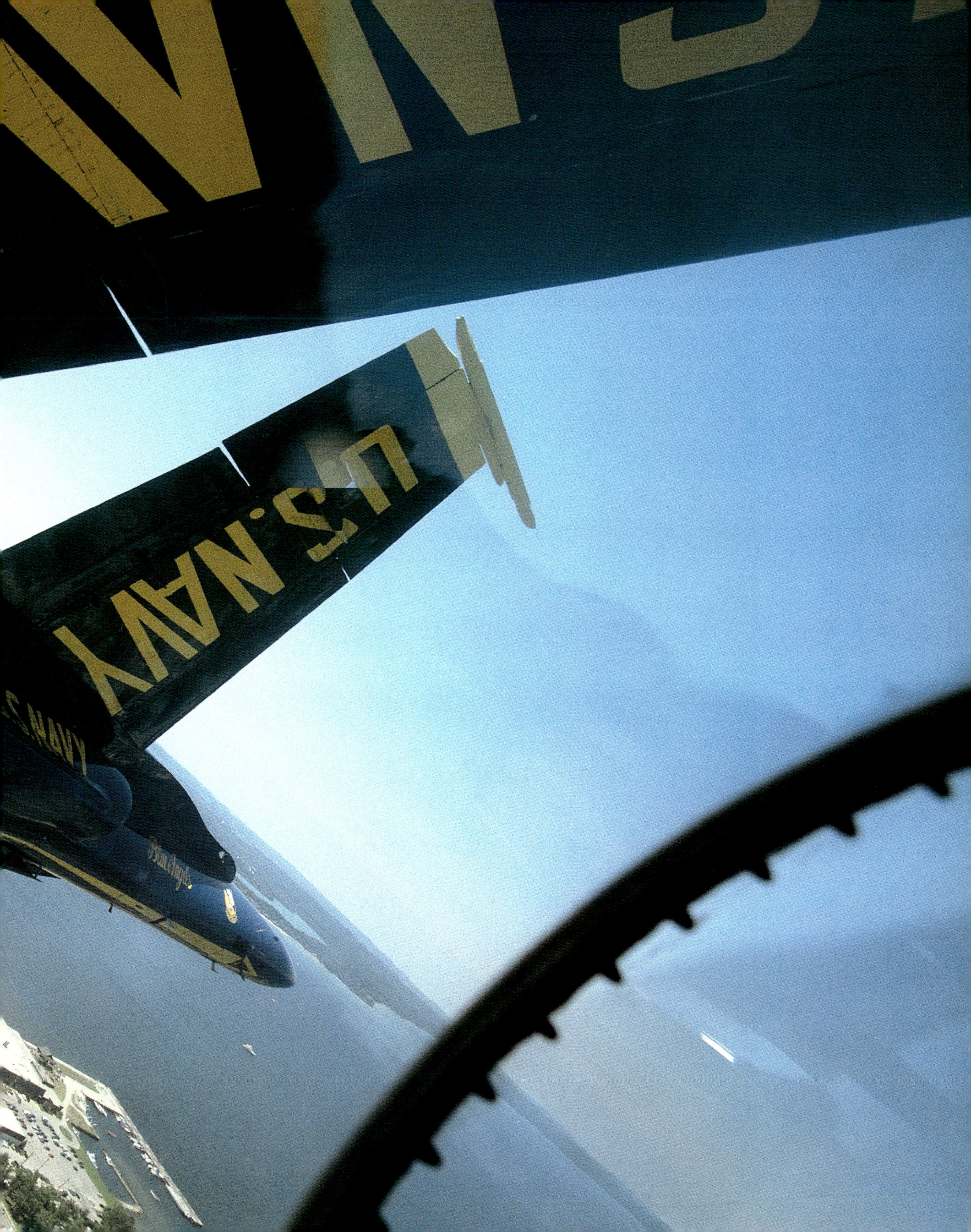
U.S. NAVY

100 BLUE ANGELS *A Portrait of Gold*

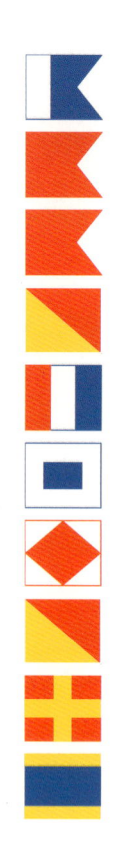

Two solos mirror each other beautifully at the completion of the Double Tuck-Over Roll.

6 Western Tour

Abbotsford, Canada

✈✈✈✈ Daddy firmly holds the microphone to his mouth, and facing an anxious air show crowd, calmly states, "These are not daring stunts, but rather maneuvers representative of those used by Navy fighter pilots throughout the fleet." While that may theoretically be true, I sense that none of the 110,000 spectators really believe him. This is Abbotsford, and those are the Blue Angels. To a crowd filled with anticipation, this *is* the daring team. To many, the Blues invented aerial daring. Who else flies the Diamond Dirty Loop, does a Double Tuckover Roll in section, and defies all formation convention with the Double Farvel? No one. And when these men in blue have flown their routine and smartly climb from their jets, wearing no G-suits, they are far from what anyone thinks are average fighter pilots performing "representative maneuvers." And the crowd wants it no other way.

Most of the people in this part of the country need no introduction to the Blues, having seen them perform here during past air show seasons. Celebrating its 33rd annual show, Abbotsford is an air show rich with tradition, and the people here know how to make it an event. These are the folks, who during the Blues' legendary Phantom era, actually invited both the Thunderbirds and the Blue Angels to Abbotsford to fly their F-4s in the same show. Such practices are not allowed today, but those who witnessed it still cherish the memory of that spectacle, when daring roared to new heights.

Abbotsford is what an air show should be – continuous flying acts throughout the day. It is truly an international event, with Air Force A-10s from both Alaska and Arizona, F-4Gs from the Idaho Air National Guard, Canadian F-5s, assorted vintage planes from the Confederate Air Force, F-16s and F-15s, several civilian plane demonstrations, and even the Goodyear blimp. There is rarely a moment when there is not something to watch overhead, ensuring many sunburned faces at days end. Canada's own flight demonstration team, the Snowbirds, will fly the final act, closing the show with an impressive variety of formations.

But in the midst of such air show splendor, it is the Blue Angels' performance which sees the massive crowd bunch most noticeably toward the runway area. As #7's litany of narration signals the beginning of the Blues' routine, and thousands of eager spectators press against three miles of wooden snow fence, it is evident that this is the act they came most to see. Among many other fine performances, this is one of the very few which commands the attention of other experienced air show performers, as they too stop what they are doing and huddle around their own planes to watch the Blues fly. Do not tell this crowd it is not daring.

Abbotsford Air Show Pavilion

✈✈✈✈ The weather at Abbotsford has frequently been a problem in the past, but the sun shines brightly this year for the entire air show weekend. A pavilion has been set up for the air show performers, and large spreads of food are put out for them each show day. Blue Angel maintenance personnel relax in the shade of the tented area, and enjoy a momentary break from their busy morning. The pilots are just arriving, and will begin briefing soon in a nearby trailer. The maintenance crews have been here since 0630, prepping the jets for the day's performance. They will still be out here when the show is completed and the pilots begin the debriefing. For now, they enjoy being treated to lunch and take a well-earned break.

I watch Lawman get some fruit from the food table, and take time to talk with the crew chiefs. The bond that these men have formed over the year can only be understood by those who have worked this closely and have traveled this much together. Lawman is a different person from the man I first saw sitting in the briefing room at Luke months ago. Somewhat more confident, he seems to be enjoying the year a little more.

Lawman is an admirable example of a "first year guy" on this team. He has been through the sternest of tests in the past eight months, and through it all, has never lost his courteous manner, his enthusiasm, and the ability to laugh at himself. Given the tests he has faced daily, this has been no easy task.

As the sole new guy in the diamond, Lawman has received more concentrated criticism, critique, and instruction than he ever thought he could absorb. Every man's pride is assaulted when he is new to flying as a Blue Angel, especially during the brutal learning process of winter training season. Lawman has endured nothing different from what the others experienced in their first year – he simply has done it alone. There were times when he seriously began to doubt himself.

Recounting those winter days, he remarks, "There were times when I would be driving home, hands so weak I was barely able to grip the steering wheel, and would wonder why in the world they picked me for the team at all."

Winter training is the great equalizer for all Blue Angel pilots. For the "new guy," there are no long sit-down sessions with the man he is replacing, no detailed instructional flights with his predecessor to ensure he is grasping every subtlety of the position's movements. He is simply put on the wing of one of the experienced members, and he starts flying. There, he will get used to staying in position while fighting the unrelenting pressures of a stick that after 20 minutes soon resembles the fatigue of reeling in a 200 pound marlin. Early training flights will last over an hour with several time-outs being issued for new pilots, in order to ease aching forearms and shake some blood back into fingers numbly trying to grasp the stick. After only ten sorties like this, the intensity is stepped up as four planes are brought together to form the diamond.

In the bleak setting of the southern California desert, these chosen few will be put through a minimum of 120 training sorties flown in 10 of the most challenging weeks in any pilots' career. Separated from their families, in the confines of El Centro, California, the team will get down to the severe task of building a formation. As brutally exhausting as the flights are, the lengthy debriefings can be worse. Twice a day, six days a week, this routine will continue, and will humble all who desire to wear the Blue Angel crest.

Not everyone can do this, even when they think they can. There is no grace period, no room for continued errors, and luck ceases to be a luxury. Regardless of a man's past accomplishments or reputation, the formation is consistent in its unforgiving nature. It is serious business learning to fly the Blue Angel way. Only those who have done it truly know the level of intensity, and courage required. During the 1967 winter training season, Lieutenant Frank Gallagher was killed when his Tiger jet struck the desert floor near El Centro; 17 days later, his replacement, Captain Ron Thompson, died the same way.

On rare occasions, a pilot is removed from the team during winter training in the interest of safety. There is no shame; it is simply a performance guided decision. There are no compromises at 400 knots, less than three feet apart. The team would rather face the difficult decision of dismissing a team member, than have to deal with the finality of attending his funeral – or their own.

Lawman survived it, but not without digging deep within himself, both mentally and physically. In addition to being the one Marine and the new guy in the diamond, Lawman was also the only one with no prior F/A-18 experience. Showing up at winter training with 30 hours in the jet and no air show experience was intimidating to say the least. This was as steep a mountain as anyone would want to climb, and Lawman's foremost goal initially was simply "not to hit the Boss." In the process, his greatest desire was to earn the respect and trust of his teammates, that he knew only comes with solid, proven performance.

WESTERN TOUR

103

LAW – MAN

Watching Lawman munch on an apple as he relaxed with Blues enlisted members at the pavilion, he seems far removed from the pressures that he has endured this year. Recalling the shows at Beaufort Marine Air Station, and El Toro, Lawman recounts, "There I am representing the entire Marine Corps, flying an airplane I am still getting acquainted with, in front of some of the hottest F/A-18 jocks in the Corps, and I can just feel their eyes on me. But it really didn't bother me too much, since I knew that Dino's eyes were on me even more." As Lawman breaks into a laugh, he seems clearly in control of handling the trials of his first year.

Lawman is no stranger to the emotions of handling severe stress. Leading a flight of two Harriers into battle during Desert Storm, his flight was maneuvering at low altitude, to avoid marginal weather, when they began taking enemy fire. His wingman, and best friend, was shot down that day, and was listed as Missing In Action for several weeks. Lawman led several flights attempting to locate his friend's position in case he was still alive, but to no avail. Eventually, the downed pilot's body was recovered and identified. Lawman volunteered for the unenviable duty of escorting his friend's casket back to the States. After a long emotion-filled journey, he faced his friend's wife and family, sadly reporting to them the details of their Marine's last known moments. As difficult as this was, Lawman felt it was his duty. He has always felt strongly about responsibility.

Prior to joining the Navy, Lawman worked as a full-time Arizona Highway Patrolman (thus, the name), and came face to face with the destruction and death caused by alcohol and narcotics on the highway. As a Blue Angel, he is emphatic in his talks to young people about the dangers of these vices and sets an example as well, having given up drinking long ago.

As Lawman gets up from lunch to head over to the briefing room and prepare himself for another performance, I can't help but feel that this man, very short in stature, stands very tall as a Blue Angel, and is, in the Boss' words, "one tough Marine."

Abbotsford Briefing

♦♦♦♦ Mo reports that all the jets are well, and this is a welcome message for the pilots. Lately, there has been a slight problem with the throttle linkage in the Boss' jet. The Leader's plane is rigged with an artificial stop to throttle movement in the full afterburner range, which precludes him from reaching full afterburner power. This ensures that the wingmen will always have at least a little power advantage when Boss pushes his throttles full forward. The Boss is happy to hear Mo's comments as no one likes having to fly the spare jet in a performance if they can help it.

Lawman and Snooze are recounting some minor flaw in Lawman's position during an echelon formation yesterday. At this stage in the season, Lawman is starting to see more in each maneuver, and is more cognizant of the small movements occurring. As #2, his movements in the echelon formations are critical, as their affect will be compounded dramatically for #3 and #4. Lawman has worked hard on smoothing out his movements in this formation, knowing that the two highly experienced men following in a line behind him are betting their lives on his consistency, and will know every time he even breathes hard.

As the pilots talk quietly around the table, the composed mood of the room is pierced by Snooze's exclamation of "WHAT? WHAT DID YOU SAY?" Apparently, in their discussion, Lawman unwittingly uses the expression, "It felt OK."

Pouncing on Lawman in mock rage, and feigning indignant horror, Snooze decries, "IT FELT OK? YOU ARE NOT A SOLO PILOT, YOU DO NOT FEEEELLL – YOU SEEEE! YOU SEEEE THE MOVEMENT, WHICH AFFECTS YOUR FRIENDS, NUMBER THREE AND NUMBER FOUR. DID WE NOT GO OVER THIS LAST WEEK?" The Boss looks up from his show notes, and can only offer Lawman a sympathetic smile. Suppressing laughter, Lawman sheepishly acknowledges his grievous error in language, and silently takes heart in Snooze's good-natured handling of this important lesson, since it is a sure sign of Lawman's progress in earning the complete trust and respect of those flying next to him.

Trust is truly the cornerstone upon which the diamond is built. Following the tirade, Dino broadly grins approval at Snooze, needing to add nothing, and can only be thinking what a fine #4 Snooze will make next year. As Lawman gets better, so do they.

Abbotsford Flightline

✦✦✦✦ Following the performance, the large crowd voices their approval with loud cheers as the team is introduced. The multitude of autograph seekers is overwhelming, but the men in blue sign as fast as their slightly numb fingers will allow. There comes a point when the pilots must leave the crowd, pose for some picture-taking sessions by the jets, and then head to debrief. The responsibility for ensuring this movement occurs falls squarely on the shoulders of the PAO. This is one of the hardest things for Cubby to do – to tell the enthused spectators that the pilots must now leave the crowd line for other commitments. He hates being the bad guy, but knows that it has to be done, and that the pilots are counting on him to ensure it is. Cubby gets soft a few times, though, and can't seem to say "no" to the little kids asking for just one more signature. Mostly he is firm, however, in this unenjoyable task, and sees to the pilots' movement over to the planes where other special groups are also waiting patiently.

✦✦✦✦ The team will stay out west this week instead of returning to Pensacola, since California's Miramar Naval Air Station is next up on the show schedule. They look forward to a week in San Diego and are in the kind of relaxed mood that makes for a good performance as they prepare to fly their final routine at Abbotsford.

Unseasonably warm temperatures bring a record crowd for the final day at Abbotsford, and the Blues perform magnificently. Enjoying the show amidst the quiet of a grassy area off the far end of the runway, I acquire a whole new perspective of the Blues' performance from that which I had seen and heard at show center. When the solos run up their engines prior to takeoff, the steady roar agitates a flock of large birds near the runway. Quickly joining into their own winged formation, the birds perform a hurried takeoff and rise above the acrid smell of smoke oil drifting in the breeze. Further away, near the grove of pine trees lining the airfield boundary, people huddle tightly on the roof of a log cabin, reveling in their unique view of the approach patterns of Blue Angel jets that pierced the quiet of the nearby wilderness, menacingly close overhead. Using the blue Canadian sky as their canvas, sunlit Hornets brush iridescent strokes of white across a backdrop of rolling green hills and distant snowy peaks, creating a scene as powerful as it was picturesque. Near show's end when six Blue Angels pull skyward in the Delta formation, far from the crowd, the thundering echo of their collective sound can be heard reverberating against Mount Baker and its surrounding summits, applause-like in its resonance, as if the massive peaks approve heartily of the performance.

✦✦✦✦ Following their last debriefing in Abbotsford, the Blues exit the trailer in time to see the Snowbirds completing the final act of the show. In the late afternoon sun, they stop, and watch with keen interest, as the Canadians put nine tiny jets together in a very creative array of formations. It is somewhat ironic to hear these accomplished flyers make a comment that had been heard many times earlier in the day: "That's simply amazing."

Miramar Naval Air Station

Home of the Top Gun School, Miramar is the Navy's FIGHTERTOWN, USA. The air show here is on the scale of El Toro, very massive, and once again, the Blue Angels are the culminating act. This year marks the 40th anniversary of Miramar and with the transfer of the Top Gun School imminent, the base has gone all out to make it a show to remember.

✦✦✦✦ The team is really starting to come together and in a particularly good mood this weekend. They've had a good trip out west so far. Some of the perks of being a Blue Angel were seen during the week as they went sailing with the America's Cup Yacht Team, attended a San Diego Chargers preseason football game, and were guests at Gold's Gym for their workouts. Somewhere between all that, they managed to get in their practice flights.

BLUE ANGELS *A Portrait of Gold*

I sense that the team is really up for this particular show, though no one verbalizes it. The obvious scrutiny from their peers, especially those instructing at the Top Gun School, cannot be dismissed as an added incentive to perform well. No one on the team admits to any such thing, saying this show is approached like every other one, and they will, as always, try to fly their best. A fine answer, but I am unconvinced. I know all too well that the adage, "Better to die than look bad," is part of every fighter pilot's psyche in some form. I sense they are taking this show very seriously – something about peer pressure here.

During one of the practice briefings, Zeke Cormier is invited to sit in with the team. A former Blue Angel Leader, Zeke led the team during the 1954-1956 seasons, before most of the pilots in the room were even born. Nevertheless, they welcome him like an important family relation, and he joins them only after ensuring that he is not disrupting their prebriefing routine in any way.

It is particularly interesting to watch the Boss sit and talk with the man who held his post forty years ago. Many eager youngsters have approached the Boss this year at different shows, all visibly elated with the opportunity to speak with Blue Angel #1. The same enthusiasm was now evident on Boss' face as he too had the opportunity to speak with another Blue Angel #1. His face beamed as brightly as the many youngsters whose lives he had touched this year, as he indulged in the chance to learn more about the Blue Angel history of which he was now a part.

Naval Training Center, San Diego

Friday mornings prior to air show weekends are normally reserved for community service by team members. They will use this time to visit and give talks to a variety of schools, hospitals, and civic groups that have been set up by the Events Coordinator months earlier. Sometimes they will be accompanied by the local Navy recruiter, thus enhancing his ability to interest young people in Navy careers. These visits are not only made by the pilots, but by other support officers and enlisted Blue Angels, who also take an active part in these important presentations.

Later, in the afternoon, a practice show will be flown for special guests of the air show sponsors, such as disabled children, veterans groups, and terminally ill youngsters in the Make-A-Wish Program.

♦♦♦♦ At 0800, on Friday morning, #5 and his crew chief meet in the hotel lobby awaiting an officer from the nearby Naval Training Center. The center is host to a program for young people called DEFY – Drug Education For Youths – and today Hoops will be speaking to the group and showing a short Blue Angel video.

Currently in his third year with the team, Hoops is the lead solo pilot. Consequently, he's given many of these types of talks before, and he relishes the opportunity to do so now. Hoops realizes that he'll have a chance to reach more kids this way, and as a Blue Angel, he will have more of a lasting impact on them than most adults would.

An imposing figure in his blue flight suit, Hoops, even at this early hour, is already being bombarded with questions and requests from guests in the hotel lobby. Politely, he talks with everyone, even a man who asks him to wait in the lobby until the rest of the family upstairs can be retrieved for an autograph session. (Where's Cubby when you really need him?) Hoops' crew chief quickly gives the man some Blue Angel handouts, tells him to bring the family to the show later where they can get everyone's signature, and points out the staff car just then arriving at the hotel. The man is happy and thanks them for the handouts. Hoops and his chief exchange a high five on the way out the door. These folks are a team.

♦♦♦♦ One can never fully prepare for the kind of wonderful questions that the DEFY kids ask, such as "Who invented the Blue Angels?" After viewing the tape that showed, from a cockpit camera, the effects of G forces on the pilot, a kid asks, "Why did your face look all funny there, and does that cool music play in your headphones all the time?" There is even one for the crew chief from a young man who wanted to know how the chief had learned to build Blue Angel jets. And of course, the inevitable "How did you become a Blue Angel?"

When Hoops explained, "Well, when I was younger, I didn't know whether I wanted to be a pilot or a farmer," it surprised the kids. To them, the thought of this superhero with the cool flight suit almost ending up a wheat farmer in North Dakota made them stop and think. They listened.

Hoops nearly did end up raising wheat, or cattle, but took a year off from school and followed his yearnings, straight to the noisy cockpit of a crop duster. Inexperienced, but eager to learn, he took every job his boss would allow him to fly. Bouncing a wing off the ground one day did not deter him from completing his dusting assignment, and only upon landing, did he realize the extent of the damage to the crushed wing tip. He worked the rest of the summer to pay off the damages in full, but kept his craving for the challenge he found in flying. Eventually, the Air Force seemed the way to go – but they turned down his application due to a bad knee. Persisting, he had surgery to repair the knee. He then applied to the Navy and was accepted for flight training.

By the time Hoops became a Top Gun instructor, he had learned much since his crop dusting days, and had helped train some of the Navy's best fighter pilots. Watching the Blue Angels perform one day, he wondered, like most fighter pilots do, if he was good enough to fly like that. For Hoops, the Blue Angels represented yet one more challenge to conquer. He was turned down the first time he applied for the team. Undeterred, he applied again. Once selected, he found himself as team Narrator for a season, and took it as a chance to improve his public speaking skills, something he does very well today.

After watching the diamond pilots endure some very heavy debriefings during winter training, Hoops felt he would be best suited for a solo position, and moved up to #6 the following year. This is a man who has worked very hard to be good at what he does, thriving on challenges, particularly wanting to tackle those things in life that elicit initial fear.

Flying in the Navy, and especially with the Blue Angels, Hoops has been challenged every day. Reflecting on his flying career, he says, "When you sign up to fly Navy, no one really tells you what carrier ops are all about, or you might stop and really think about what you are doing; and similarly, if someone told you what Blue Angel flying was really like, you might think twice about applying." But men like Hoops will always apply, even if they are told of every danger, because the difficulty, and sometimes fear, of the thing is what makes them want to conquer it. Even when he watches the diamond fly, he admits that he still wonders if he can do that.

On the way back to the hotel, I ask Hoops if the guys are going to work out today after the practice show. He informs me that he already worked out at 0530 this morning, knowing he would have little time the rest of the day. A man driven.

Miramar Air Show

♦♦♦♦ Part of the air show day routine with this team is the process of simply getting the pilots from the hotel to the show site. To facilitate this drive, which is normally encumbered with miles of air show traffic, the Blues enlist a police escort to lead their caravan of rental cars through the maze of traffic, crowds, and special entry points to the airfield. Riding in the Blue Angel caravan is the next most stimulating experience to flying with them. Racing through city streets, the line of ten cars follows a team of enthusiastic motorcycle policemen who deftly handle the stoppage of all traffic and seem bent on impressing the team with just how quickly they can deliver them to the airfield.

With two feet of wing tip *-correction, bumper-* clearance, the pilots fly *-drive-* with one arm out the window to flash hand signals so that everyone knows when to apply speedbrakes *-brakes-* as they zoom *-that's zoom-* through town. Once comfortable in the formation *-caravan-* the enjoyable part is watching the enthused faces of the people along the way, as they realize who it is the police are escorting. Even those being held at intersections by the flashing red lights of the escort wave and smile as they recognize the Blue Angel flight suits on the flyers *-drivers-* passing them. This is good, since the caravan to Miramar closed down all four northbound lanes of I-15 temporarily. The caravan is a little like being in a parade, albeit a very fast parade.

Prior to strapping on *-getting into-* the cars for the trip to Miramar, a group of special guests of the team talk with the pilots who congregate in the parking lot. Some members of the San Diego Chargers have been invited to ride along today in appreciation for their hospitality during the week. Timber and Hoops are giving Cubby some heat over, well, just being Cubby. Just hours ago, they were working out together in the weight room as pals. Now, well, it's air show time, and what a great opportunity to let our pal Cubby know how much we like him by firing some shots his way. "Yes Cubby," says Timber, "your spot in the caravan is at the very end, and will always be at the end – AS IT SHOULD BE."

Cubby is used to this perverse fighter pilot humor by now, and would only worry if it were any other way. He has learned that this is just the pilots' way of releasing the tension and apprehension that is always present before flying a big show. When they are in the air, few people watch the show as intently and hope for its safe completion as much as their pal Cubby.

This is a tough week for Cubby as this is a Navy town, and that means increased numbers of VIPs, Navy brass, and other military groups that will require some of his attention. Otter has come along on this trip to help relieve Cubby of some of the administrative duties this show always entails.

One of the guests, a woman who has chatted at length with most of the pilots, finally makes her way to the tall, somber looking man slightly squinting from the morning sun, and espies the gold #4 sewn on his flight suit. Approaching him cautiously, she initiates conversation with "I hear you are the coolest guy on the team, and fly the most difficult position." Dino, motionless, looks at her, and ever so slowly breaks into his patent grin, replying, "No ma'am, I actually fly the coolest position, and am the most difficult guy." Then he breaks out with that big grin that lets you know what a softie he really is.

Miramar Briefing

✤✤✤✤ The briefing room is filled with snacks donated by base well-wishers. The large plate stacked with chocolate chip cookies in the center of the table is tempting, and I reach for one. Snooze, with the stare of mock anger normally reserved for Lawman, asks, "Did YOU work out this morning?" I carefully put the cookie back, another mistake. Snooze adds, "You expect us to eat a cookie you've fondled? You just bought yourself a $5 cookie, mister." When the Boss sits down and takes a cookie, then everyone can have one, sort of like the smoking lamp being lit. I had momentarily forgotten the basic precept of this organization – TEAM. But I felt good, like Lawman had at times, that I could be reminded in this particular manner, since I knew it was reserved for those with whom they had become comfortable.

Timber watches a Harrier jet flying outside, and remarks to Lawman, "Hey, there's one of those 'Scarier' jets doing weird things out there." In a rare return volley, Lawman politely replies that it is only scary to those who couldn't handle a real man's jet. A minor milestone for Lawman, but a subtle indication that the team is solidifying. They are starting to peak as a group, and as I bite into my $5 cookie, I anticipate a good show today.

Timber, a Top Gun School graduate, flew the F-14 here at Miramar, and is quite proud to return now as a Blue Angel solo pilot. He always wanted to fly with the Blues. For most Navy pilots, after experiencing carrier ops, being selected for Top Gun training, or flying in combat, flying with the Blue Angels is the final challenge left. "When people come to this team," states Timber, "they often find it a larger leap than anticipated." Like most selectees to the Blues, Timber represents the very best in Navy flying, one of the "water-walkers," as they are jokingly described. "But," he says, "when you get here, you basically have to start all over again. It's not that you can't fly the maneuvers, it's learning to fly them with the degree of precision required."

Timber, like Hoops, also started as Narrator on the team and felt that flying a solo position would be more satisfying than those "unhappy winter diamond debriefs." He says, "I respect those guys a lot, but I definitely don't suffer from diamond envy. As a solo I get to fly the jet the way I've always wanted." Far more forgiving than the F-14, the Hornet impresses Timber with its ability to maneuver in ways he wasn't used to in the Tomcat.

110 BLUE ANGELS *A Portrait of Gold*

TOP
Timber settles in for another day at the office.

BOTTOM
Following the diamond Tuck-Under Break, all three wingmen rejoin to the Leader. As seen from #3's jet, Lawman proceeds to rejoin with the Boss, just out of view.

Getting really comfortable flying a precise ground track at 200 feet while inverted was one of Timber's greatest challenges at the start of the year: "I had to do that many, many times, before it started to become second nature."

An interesting challenge for Timber next year will be learning to fly all the solo maneuvers he's not flying now, as he will move up to lead solo and fly a different show routine. One of the rare people on the team who is actually looking forward to winter training, Timber already is formulating ideas about how to make minor improvements to the solo routine next season.

Together, Timber and Hoops make a formidable pair, bringing much experience and talent to the solo portions of the demonstration. Watching them sitting around the table now, they have the definite look of quiet confidence.

Miramar Flightline

✦✦✦✦ The Blues' performance is one of the best of the year. There is no denying the team was up for this one. My suspicions were correct. Though they would still probably deny it, they appeared to fly tighter, lower, and harder than normal. Even Bert flew more aggressively today, getting his nose a little higher in the climb and ripping across the parked Hornets with extra knots gleaned from somewhere inside that "sleek" Hercules.

Somehow, Timber managed to squeeze an extra vertical roll, or two, out of that Hornet at the top of his corkscrew of white smoke. And he looked rock solid at just under 200 feet, as he and Hoops raced past the ramp of Top Gun Tomcats, inverted. And maybe, just maybe, there was a missile rail's width between the diamond planes as they flew that 360 tighter than should be possible, moving across show center like a single piece of sculpted blue metal. And when Hoops brought his screaming jet low, and in close to the crowd line for the sneak pass, pockets of white condensation were ripped from his accelerating wings as the shock wave across his plane moved teasingly aft. And Hoops nudged the Mach, and 200,000 spectators collectively jumped as they unexpectedly found an angry blue Hornet in their laps. This was Miramar, home of Top Gun, where rows of Tomcats pugnaciously echoed "Anytime, baby," and some of the fleet's best were watching with the same keen eyes used to hunt the "bandit." The team knew; regardless of everything they didn't say this week...they knew.

Hoops was long past the crowd line as the sharp echo of his 'burners pummeled the FIGHTERTOWN, USA hangar one more time. As the crowd collected themselves following the sneak pass, everyone seemed genuinely glad that the Blues were in town for the weekend. At that moment, I was simply glad that Hoops had decided not to become a farmer.

BLUE ANGELS *A Portrait of Gold*

TOP
With a "Reeeaaddy HIT IT!" call, the solos meet at show center in a violent flash of wings in the Inverted-to-Inverted Pass.

BOTTOM
Hoops races across the crowd line with the attention-getting Sneak Pass. As the crowd is directed to look to the right, Hoops speeds in from the left and shocks the spectators with his high speed pass.

WESTERN TOUR 113

*TOP
The Echelon Parade Pass. Stacked in echelon formation, each man is counting on those in front of him to remain stable.*

*BOTTOM
On takeoff, Timber sets the stick in his lap and squeezes moisture from the humid air.*

114 BLUE ANGELS *A Portrait of Gold*

Flying is only one part of the job, and Cubby watches attentively as a local TV station interviews Hoops. A day later, Hoops talks with kids in the DEFY program.

WESTERN TOUR 115

TOP
The JATO takeoff, as seen looking back from the fuselage of Bert. Below are the Miramar runways, masses of spectators, and six blue jets.

BOTTOM
Once Bert has landed, the crew chiefs and pilots stand ready to begin the main show.

116　　　　　　　　　　　　　　　　　　　　　　　　　　　　　　　　**BLUE ANGELS** *A Portrait of Gold*

Blue Angel maintenance crews are some of the hardest working people on the air show circuit, performing a myriad of tasks to keep those jets ready.

OVERLEAF
The
Diamond
360 is
the most
photographed
of all
Blue Angel
formations.
This
rendition at
Miramar was
one of the
best ever.

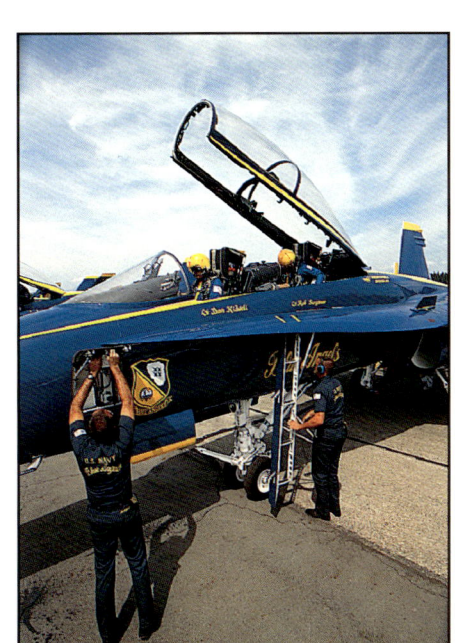

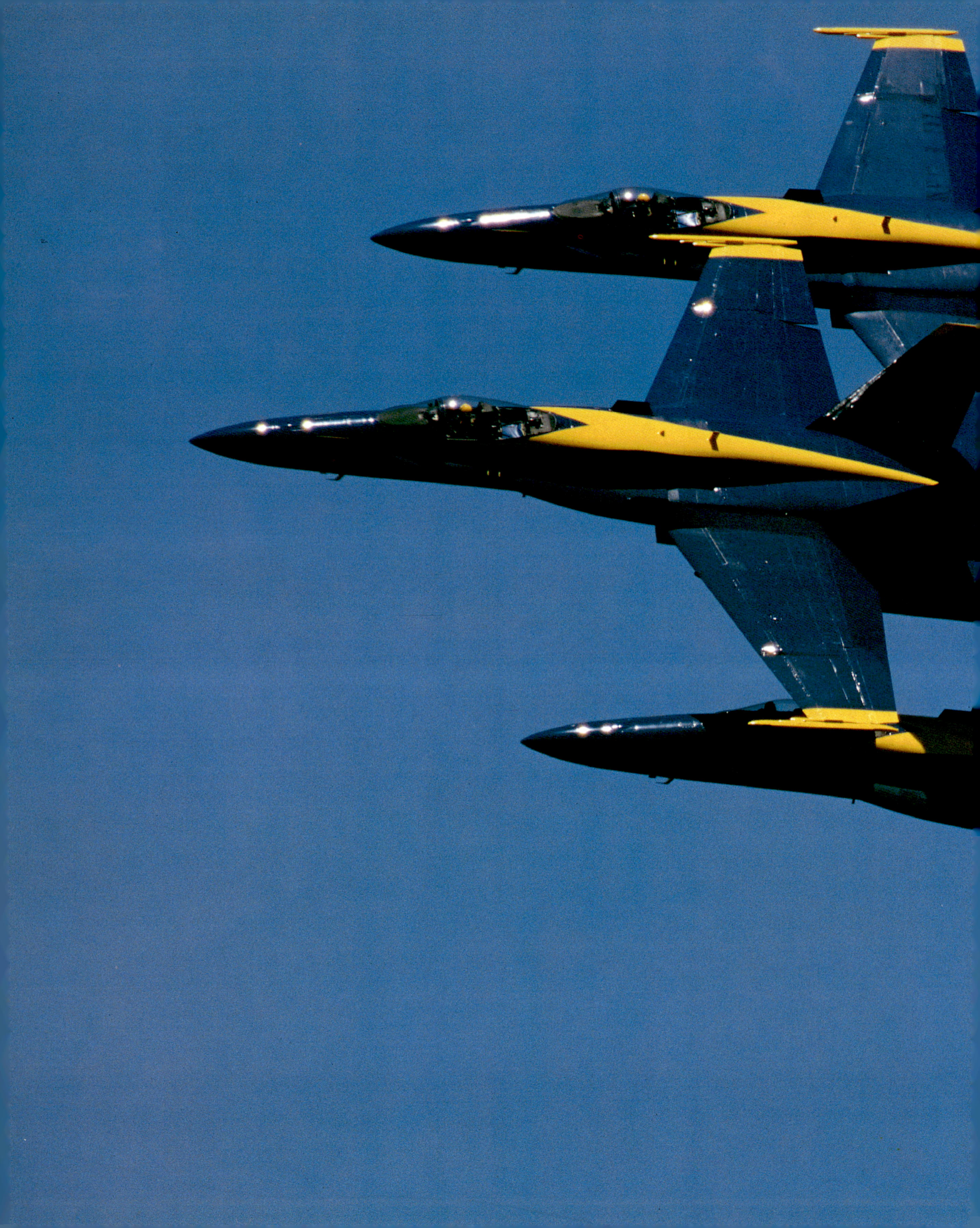

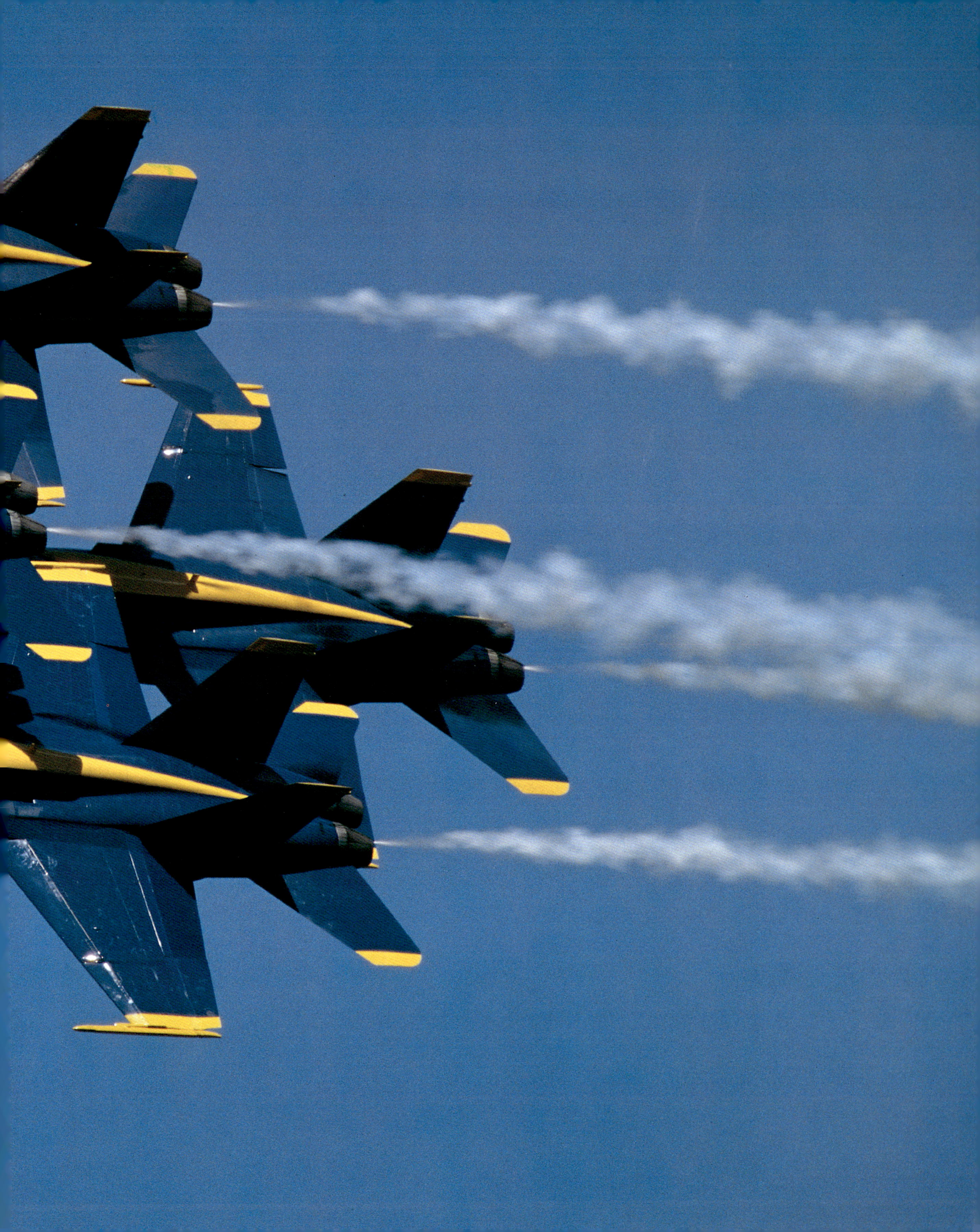

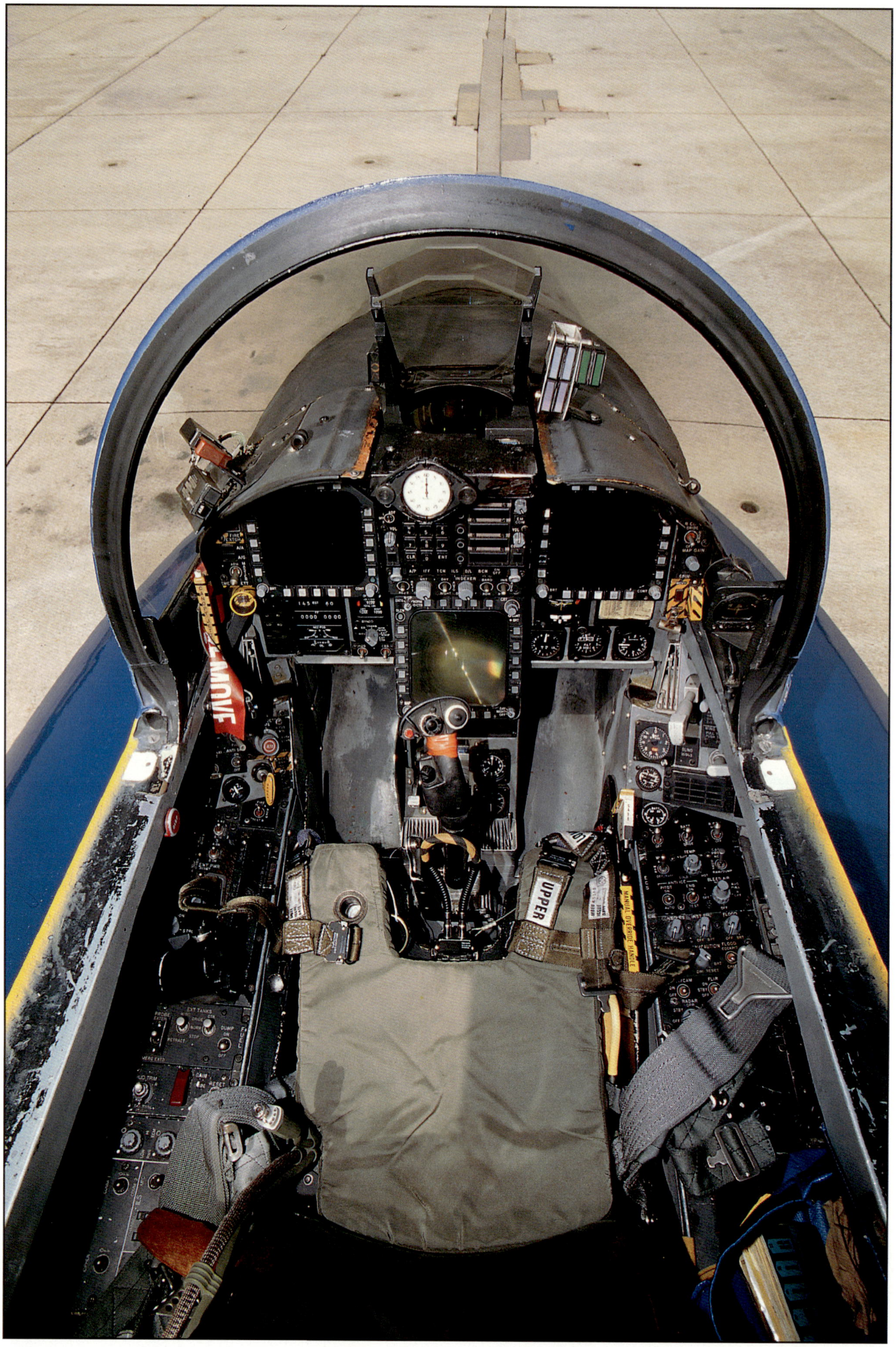
UPPER

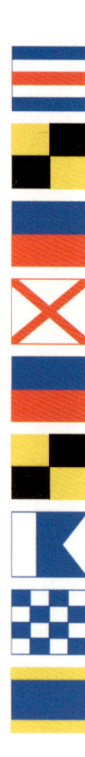

7 The Seven Jet

Burke-Lakefront Airport, Cleveland, Ohio

✦✦✦✦ Standing on the flightline, I am trying to get an unobstructed photo of one of the parked Blue Angel jets, in order to illustrate some of the references the pilots use to stay in formation. Interestingly, the little painted hornet on the fuselage is used to help them align their position off the wing in close formation. When a pilot is involved in the effort of staying in precise position on the wing, it is referred to as "workin' the bug." On the left side of the planes leading edge extension, above the last step into the cockpit, there are two painted lines that resemble two captain's bars. These lines help the pilot to guide his foot into the recessed first step when exiting the cockpit. These "bars" are also used as an in-flight reference, especially in aligning the Line-Abreast Loop. An additional corresponding single stripe was added to the right side of the plane. This stripe, called "the cigarette," serves the same purpose. Even the painted words "McDonnell Douglas" and "Blue Angels" on the fuselage sides provide reference points for the pilots. The squadron crest is the only emblem on the fuselage not used for an alignment reference.

As maintenance folks continue to perform a variety of functions, on, in, and around the planes, I am left only with the #7 jet unencumbered with servicing requirements. The two-seater is not the one I want to photograph, as the larger canopy looks ungainly, and it is not one of the six main show birds. I leave the plane and head for the briefing room where the pilots have gathered.

✦✦✦✦ Sitting against the wall with Otter and Heyjoe, we hear Mo inform Dino that his jet has a problem, and it's serious. He'll have to fly the #7 jet in today's show. Dino just nods as he finishes his lunch of potato salad and chicken. In a moment, Dino turns from the briefing table, looks squarely at me, and states in a direct tone, "You're flying with me today; get your stuff."

Using the back end of an empty Fat Albert, I rapidly change into a flight suit, stuffing film into zippered pockets. At this point in the season, I've gotten used to flying without a G-suit, and my G tolerance has finally caught up to the show routine. Increased workouts with the team have left me feeling as strong as when I flew A-10 demo flights at this same air show, years earlier. My previous flights with the team had always been scheduled ahead of time, but this was the first time they made a spontaneous decision to fly me, and I felt good about that. I knew this meant I had earned a measure of trust with them at their place of work – in the cockpit.

In the briefing

✦✦✦✦ An extra seat has been added around the briefing table. When you fly, you sit at the table. The briefing begins on time. Initially, the Boss goes around the table, and each pilot briefly states their flying goals for the day. This "confessional" helps to keep everyone equally humbled, and it reinforces the work ethic required to approach this intense level of flying.

Lawman, *quietly:* "Yessir, Boss, I'm going to work hard at pushing my nose forward coming out of echelon, and improve my rejoin after the cross, definitely make it better than yesterday's, lookin' forward to havin' a good one. Glad to be here, Boss."

Snooze, *seriously:* "Good mornin' Boss, gotta clean up the Echelon Roll, and gonna line those helmets up in the Line-Abreast Loop. Glad to be here, Boss."

Dino, *slowly:* "Today, Boss, I'll leave you a little more room coming out of the Farvel, and I'll try not to drag my ass in the Dirty Loop. Let's all have a really good one. Glad to be here, Boss."

Hoops, *enthusiastically:* "Mornin' Boss. Gotta work on our timing today, and need to get rejoined to Delta a little quicker. Glad to be here, Boss."

Timber, *thoughtfully:* "Gotta get the setup better for the Fortus, workin' on keeping wings level, watchin' out for those tall buildings down there. Glad to be here, Boss."

Snooze covers the emergency procedure of the day along with divert field information. After an overview of the parking lineup, taxi routes, and the Delta maneuvers, the Boss splits the solo pilots off to a separate room, and proceeds to review with the diamond, in detail, the sequence of maneuvers. When the solos leave, so do Mo, Doc and #7 and #8, who will proceed to the comm trailer at show center. Bert's pilot, Heyjoe, leaves for the tower where he will serve as a safety observer.

Left alone in the library-like quiet of the briefing room, the diamond performs their final preparation for the show. As the Boss mentally traces his flightpath across the airfield photo in front of him, he speaks the radio calls he will make for each maneuver in the same cadence he will use in the air. As the Boss speaks, the rest of the diamond visualize their positions and movements in each maneuver described. Likewise, the solos perform a similar concentrated review of their show routine in a room down the hall. In somewhat of a meditation process, each man reinforces precisely what he is supposed to be doing at each juncture in the show sequence.

When the Boss is through, they discuss some fine points more informally. Dino points out that Boss forgot to mention a "smoke off" call. Boss acknowledges, and thanks him for pointing that out. They continually double check each other, as there is no room for mental errors. The team must fly in complete concert with each other for every second they are in the air, and must have no doubts themselves, or in each other.

In the #7 jet

♦♦♦♦ Strapping into an F/A-18 is a fairly involved process. Besides the normal survival kit connections, shoulder harness, lap belt, and radio cord, there are two additional restraint device connections for each leg. These restraints reduce the flailing that results from a high speed ejection. Additionally, the Blues have added a rugged torso restraining harness to minimize vertical body movement during inverted and negative G flight. By the time the #4 crew chief has ensured that all my connections and straps are fastened to appropriate tightness, I definitely begin to feel one with the airplane.

The pilots march down the line of jets in front of a large Cleveland crowd. The weather is spectacular, something of a rarity in this part of the country. As Dino climbs into the front seat he casually asks, "How ya doin' back there?" no differently than if we were going boating today on Lake Erie, seemingly impervious to the 80,000 people staring in our direction. As the large canopy on the #7 jet electrically closes, I hear the comforting sound of the air vent as it blows cool air across my sweating body.

Taxiing out, Dino seems glued to Snooze's wing tip, but still manages the occasional turn of his head into the cockpit without losing position. Throngs of people wave as we taxi past the long show line that has Burke-Lakefront famous.

On the runway, we set ourselves on the right side of the formation, off Lawman's right wing. With head nods, the wingmen relay to Boss that they are ready to go, and with the slamming of throttles full forward, brakes are released and our Hornet lurches forward.

Navy landing gear is built tough to withstand hard carrier landings, but it does not make for a smooth ride on the ground, and the takeoff roll is as bumpy as always.

Lifting effortlessly off the runway, four planes' wheels are raised in unison, and Dino quickly, but smoothly, slides beneath Lawman's twin tails, en route to his slot position. Once he is tucked safely between the spear-like wing tips of #2 and #3, he drives his nose forward, and slightly up, as he tucks himself precariously close to the Boss' jet wash. As we set ourselves into position, Lawman and Snooze ease in toward us as if locking us into position, and the diamond is set for the Boss to take it into the vertical for the show opening loop. It's been only moments since we have left the small boats on the lake behind.

The familiar cadence of Boss' voice on the radio signals the wingmen as to his rate of pull on the stick. In the time it takes Boss to say "Uuuup-weeee-go!" we have transitioned from a slight 1G climb to noses pointing upward in a 4G pull. It is at that moment that I feel closest to the heart of the Blue Angel experience. All mystique and reputation are brushed aside as I am immediately confronted by simultaneous increases in G force, closeness, and danger. Rushing into position and up for a loop, momentarily faster than my senses can absorb, I find my eyes riveted to the underside panels of Boss' jet. The wing tips of #2 and #3 wave like yellow batons of steel about our canopy, as if in warning – except that they go unheeded, and we continue to push forward. The moment exceeds emotions, and I find myself in the grip of a formation that heeds only to ability.

Amidst the chaotic howling of engines close by, it is an exciting moment, but I must force the signals of midair collision from my mind, and push aside the mounting sense of danger. When this combination of fear and exhilaration come together, compressed as tightly as the steady G force on the body, it is at that moment, that gloriously scary and colorful moment, when the essence of Blue Angel flying becomes as clear as the open sky we are piercing. I can watch them now, at the place where performance must conquer fear, and where only the incredible trust these men have in each other's skills enables them to walk the dangerously fine edge between the two. Death sits as close as the next airplane, and these men will see its face at least once each time they do this, holding it in check only through the countless hours of preparation they've endured to create this moment. Flying with these men during the intensity that most defines the Blue Angel experience, I feel very close to them. And though there will be much tumultuous excitation in the next forty minutes, I settle, as securely as our position in the slot, into a feeling of calm. I trust them.

♦♦♦♦ As we crest the top of the loop, Boss calls the flight out of afterburner, and the noise level drops as abruptly as the push forward in the seat from the deceleration. As the formation starts down, the sight of earth returns to the canopy, and with it brings a glorious view of the mass of people and planes coloring the Burke-Lakefront area. The few moments of relative comfort are over quickly, as the jets and pilots strain against gravity to complete the loop.

Back on the runway, the solos are performing their individual takeoff maneuvers while we now set up for the tight Diamond 360. Arcing behind the air show area, Boss lets the diamond ease their positions out, just slightly, but even this minimal change seems excessively wide from the closeness to which this team is accustomed.

Setting himself into position for the tightest formation of the day, Dino offsets slightly to the right of Boss' plane, thus creating the illusion of a more symmetrical look to the formation as it arcs in 45 degrees of bank before show center. I watch Snooze, on the inside of the turn, nudge his canopy up close to the Boss' wing until he is engulfed by the shadow from Boss' jet. Dino's shift has brought us closer to Lawman on the right wing. This move seems to split the difference between flying just below Boss' exhaust and not touching Lawman's wing tip. The scene witnessed moments earlier during the Diamond Loop seems surprisingly comfortable compared to this. Dino calmly asks, "How's this?" I am caught off guard by his question, and find that I am only able to reply "fine," uttered in a hushed tone as if any loud noise would upset the rare blue china so delicately stacked around me.

I notice the tall buildings of Cleveland below us and the waterfront area fast approaching. As I make these observations separately, I know that Dino is seeing all of it at the same time. In the midst of the left turn, Dino points out some high towers off to our right that could be a problem later in the show. There is some talking on the radio: the Boss relaying power changes to the flight, the solos confirming they are clear, Dino moving Lawman out a little. Just prior to crossing over the harbor, the excruciatingly tight formation hits a pocket of turbulence and all four planes bounce together. No one talks.

As we are getting set for the Diamond Aileron Roll, two changes take place. The diamond moves their formation out somewhat, and I move my left leg as far left as it will go. I know from experience that my leg is just large enough to take a pounding from the stick if I don't.

With a "Reeeaaady – HIT IT!" from Boss, all four planes perform a full stick deflection Aileron Roll. With the slamming of the stick full left, the roll is over in a violent half second, whereupon the three planes close quickly on Boss to reform the tight diamond, and I reposition a slightly bruised knee. As we reform for the next maneuver behind the crowd, I can't help but think about those first Blue Angel routines where the Hellcats in their little "V" formation actually rolled in a similar manner, except closer. Gutsy flying.

Below us, Hoops is straining through a 7.5G turn, impressing the crowd with the minimum turn radius in an F/A-18. Behind the crowd, the diamond is setting up for the Double Farvel. I recheck the tightness of my straps. In a few moments, we will be inverted, flying off Boss as usual, except that he will also be inverted.

At just under two miles from the runway, Dino eases out from the formation somewhat, thus giving Boss room to quickly flip his plane on its back. We do the same. Closing back in, the diamond reshapes itself, albeit uniquely. From the ground, this maneuver looks unbelievable; from the cockpit, this maneuver appears even more unbelievable. Quite disconcerting is that Boss looks normal from the slot position, but the earth and sky seem displaced. Adding to this uncomfortable feeling, the two wingmen in our view appear to be upside down – though they are actually right side up. Hanging inverted, my boots float toward the lower console, but the snug torso harness keeps my head from bumping the canopy. It does little to stop the push of blood to my head. As the anchored boat, which marks show center, passes quickly above – beneath – Boss' canopy, I know we are now in front of thousands of people getting a good view of this remarkable formation. I find the view from Dino's jet pretty remarkable.

♦♦♦♦ A little over halfway through the show, and they seem to have a good one going. #5 joins us for the Line-Abreast Loop. While simple in concept, putting five planes abreast of each other with equal spacing between all of them is quite difficult. Dino moves out of the slot and onto Snooze's left wing, as Hoops joins to Lawman's right side, consequently forming five planes abeam the Boss. With the beginning of Boss' radio cues, the five plane loop commences:

"Wings are level."

"Smoke on......Uuuuuppp-weeee-go." (Initial pull from level)

"A lit-tle more pull." (Adding more G as noses point skyward)

"Aaaaddding po-wer." (More power needed as airspeed bleeds off)

"Eas-ing the pull." (Over the top, on their backs)

"Eas-ing power...easing more power." (Noses pointing earthward)

"Standby the boards.....Boards!" (Speed brakes open)

"Comes-the-pull." (Heavy pull to recover from dive)

Once the loop is completed, Hoops drops back to rejoin Timber, and with a "Smoke off" call, the Line-Abreast Loop is complete.

From the slot, I watch the diamond transition smoothly through a variety of maneuvers, as they vividly reveal every nuance of their movements around my canopy. The radio is frequently punctuated with the sound of Dino's voice directing the formation. From this vantage point, the flow of the diamond as a whole is most dynamically evident, and I cherish my seat for this show. For some moments I am mesmerized with the sheer beauty of the scene around me, reveling in the awareness of my closeness to the very heartbeat of Blue Angel performance.

Deep into the show routine now, the diamond moves confidently to the syncopated rhythm of voice and hands, dynamically articulating their score in the symmetry of four planes moving to the same beat. Like the background bass guitarist in a small band, Dino keeps that beat moving, accompanying the melody of Boss' direction and orchestrating the diamond's movements throughout the performance. Rather than simply following at the rear of the formation, #4 pushes the diamond along.

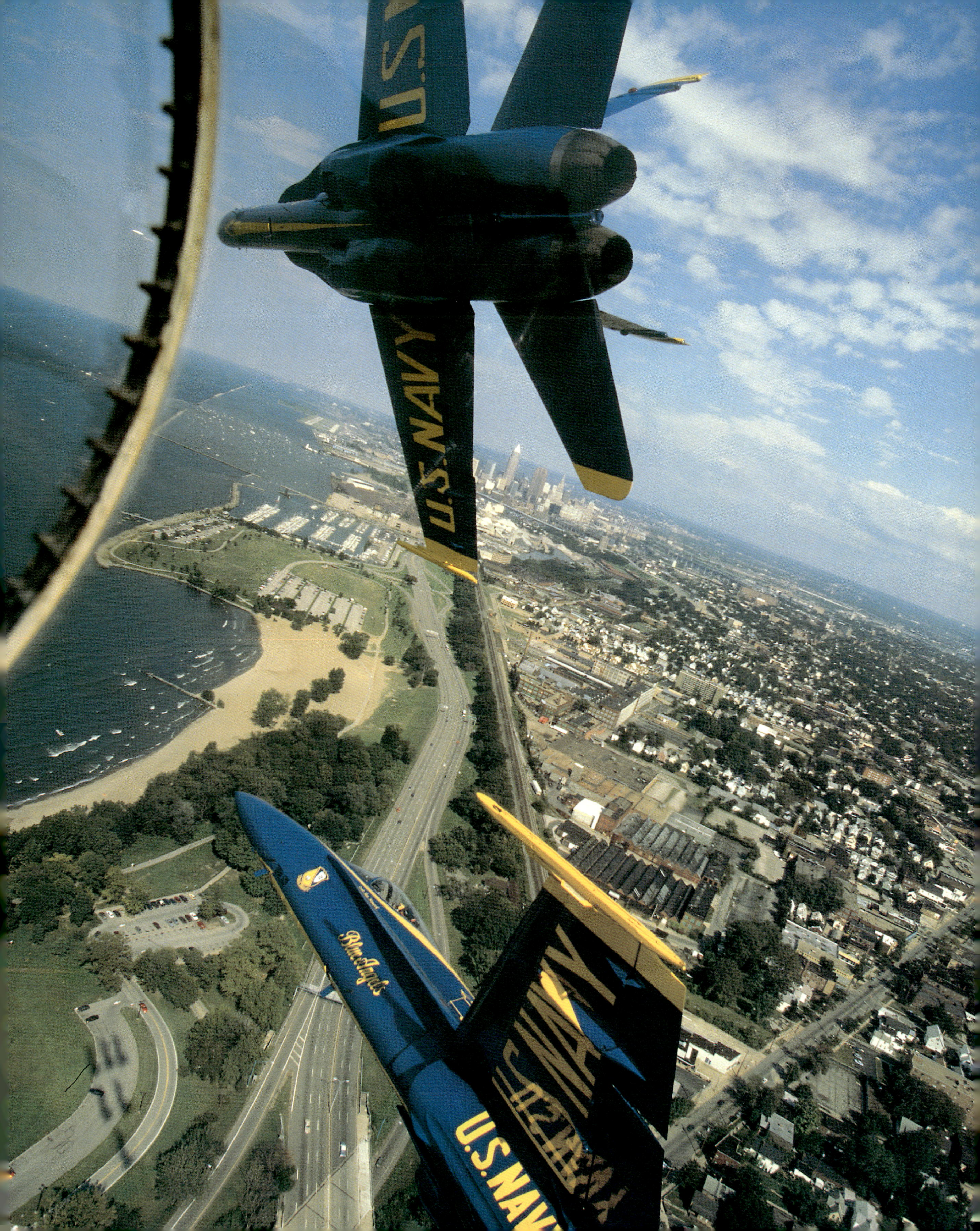
U.S.NAVY
Blue Angels

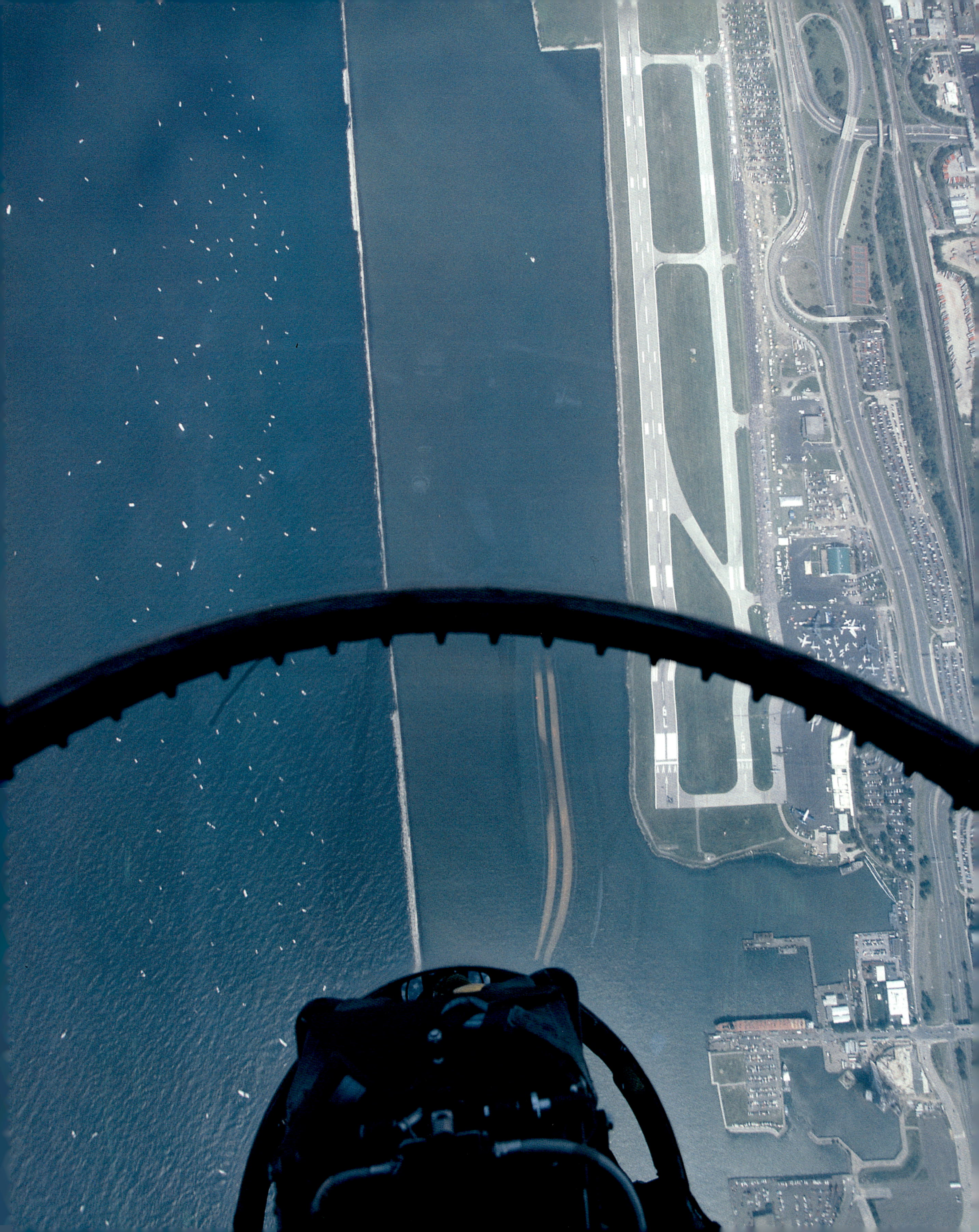

Heading straight for the crowd, the diamond is stacked in trail formation in preparation for the vertical break. Even though there are three jets in front of us, we can only see one as we are tucked closely behind #3. There is some movement as Boss pulls the formation upward. There is always some movement here, and it is always a little uncomfortable. Now, being on the tail end, it is even more noticeable. Once the formation is headed up into the vertical, Dino calls a formation change and instantly, three jets are accelerating forward on the Leader in order to reform the diamond. This movement needs to happen quickly. Once they are headed straight up, the diamond pilots will need to split immediately in four different directions. Snooze and Lawman literally charge forward to regain their respective wing positions on Boss. The rudder movement is evident on their jets as they slide to their respective sides. As if splitting them like bowling pins, Dino rolls forward confidently, assured the other two will move quickly on cue.

As the planes complete their symmetrical break, the maneuver is essentially over for the spectators on the ground, but not for the three diamond pilots. They must now rejoin rapidly, from different directions, back to their Leader. From the ground, this rendezvous maneuver is viewed with only mild interest, and appears to be routine to the average spectator for pilots such as these. This procedure may be routine in concept, but not in practice. It involves some of the most aggressive maneuvering the diamond pilots will perform all day. Above are three planes racing toward the Boss at angles and speeds that are, from a pilot's view, let us say, attention-getting.

The Boss is holding 325 knots in a gentle turn. I note our airspeed indicator is approaching 500. Usually this is not a problem, but coupled with a 60 degree heading difference, I realize that this is going to be some exciting rejoin. This rendezvous will be accomplished without the use of the speedbrake, since it is ineffective above 400 knots in this jet. As Dino scorches downtown Cleveland, racing in full 'burner to rejoin, I hear his voice in that authoritative Dino tone, "Hang on." He needn't have told me. From all I can see, I already know we are going to have to turn the proverbial "square corner" to make this work. Back in the fleet, if you botched the rejoin, you would simply under-run the Leader, sliding beneath him to the outside of his turn. In Blue Angel flying, there will be no under-runs as there are too many people making the same maneuver, and just as aggressively. I trust Dino has not misjudged his overtake, and angle off. Above us I see Lawman's jet race across our canopy with even greater angle off from Boss than we have. The white ribbons streaking from his wing tips tell me he is deep into his pull in the process of rapidly fixing the geometry. At the last moment, Dino corrects ours by throwing the jet hard into a 7G bank, effectively using the entire plane as a speedbrake. As we slide into position, this pull feels as if someone has laid an F/A-18 across my chest for several excruciating seconds. Snooze has made a similarly aggressive move with his jet, and amidst wing flashes and some heavy breathing, another routine rendezvous is completed and the diamond is reformed.

✦✦✦✦ With the call, "You've got six, Boss," the solos have let Boss know that they have joined up with the formation to form the Delta portion of the show. Pulling the large formation up for the Delta Loop Break, Dino is slightly aft of his normal position now, thus balancing the symmetry of the Delta formation. I can see Hoops close by on our left, and Timber out to the right. Pulled from the freedom of their solo routines, they are now busy "workin' the bug," and "flyin' the paint." As the formation starts back down, Boss calls for "smoke on" and gives the signal for the formation to break. Pulling six white ribbons in different directions, each plane proceeds out on a specific heading, performs a vertical repositioning maneuver, and then heads back toward show center for the six plane cross. This is an imprecise maneuver at best, but even with all the variables at work today, the team manages to get six jets crossing together in an impressive display of timing.

As the planes perform the break, we quickly find ourselves at 3400 feet, pointed earthward in 80 degrees of dive..... Dino promptly be...aauuurghhhh...gins..... a..... h...e...a...v...yyyy..... aauuurghhhh..... puulllll..... on..... t...h...e..... uuhhuuook...ssss...t...i...c...k..... and..... in..... a..... feww.....mo-ments, we-are-level, flying outbound, from, wheeeeww, the.....aaahhhh.....runway. "You couldn't do that in an A-7," remarks Dino. Nope, not from that altitude, pointing straight at the ground.

This performance is just another impressive display of this jet's muscle. Heading back toward show center, I pick up the other jets in the distance and notice their white lines of smoke converging like spokes on a wheel. Tough to see at first, the Boss suddenly comes right at us on the nose. The cross is over in a blur of blue hornets crossing all around us, and immediately, we be...aauurghgghh...gin..... a...hhuuookhhuuook...nother..... re..eeeeeeeeee..join..... manueverrrraauuurghhhh..... hhuuookhhuuook..... aauughghg..... "Hang on"..... eeeyyyaaauuuhhuuook... wheeeww..... "You've got six, Boss"...aaahhhh.
"How ya doin' back there?"
"Great!"
"Alllriiight."

♦♦♦♦ At show's end, the Delta formation passes in front of the reviewing stand as each plane aggressively pitches up for landing, punctuating their performance with one last max performance pull on the stick. Dino issues another "Hang on." I now know that when he says that, bad things are about to happen to my body. The pitch-up to land is a solid 7G snatching of the stick, followed immediately by a zero G push, which helps to level the plane on the downwind altitude. This maneuver is where guest flyers in the #7 jet usually black out. I did the very first time, but now I anticipate the pull and can actually "see" throughout the entire maneuver. The time in the weight rooms has been well spent. After 40 minutes of draining flight, this final crunch to the body only seems appropriate in closing the Blue Angel performance.

♦♦♦♦ As we taxi in and loosen straps that have left impressions across our bodies, I joke to Dino that he only made me flinch twice during the show. "That's OK," he replied, "I flinched four times myself." He wasn't joking.

In the debrief

♦♦♦♦ In the debriefing, there is much good-natured kidding about today's show, a clear sign that they had a pretty good one. They never say they had a good one, but their mood speaks volumes about their performance. Usually, the best barometer for how the debriefing will go is Dino's mood right after a show. He is smiling, indicating a relatively pleasant debrief.

Even Lawman, who earlier in the year had little to say, got the biggest laugh with his comments. Lawman made a pretty aggressive move on Boss today when charging from echelon back to the diamond formation, and for a moment in the air, two jets were closer than Blue Angel close. Of course, this did not go unnoticed by Dino, the man who has often repeated the necessity for Lawman's aggressiveness in that transition. He knows now that Lawman has the move down, and that he probably scared himself a little today, so not much needs to be said. Lawman will back it off a notch next time. As Boss goes around the table, similar to the briefing, each man has a chance to confess his errors. Lawman starts with his move from echelon, understating the sheer terror of the moment with "I got a little close to Boss today."

"Hold it, now," chimes Dino with that broad grin, "that's *my* job to tell you when you screw up, and hey, I thought you did a pretty good job today, so don't be trying to make up stuff, LAW-MAN." Always following with the grin. The last time Lawman had heard Dino joke with him like that was at Luke, months ago, and he knows it now signifies reaching a new, and hard earned, plateau of trust from the men who count most to him, his peers. "So tell me, Lawman, did you see the little cigarette stripe on Boss' jet?" Dino asks with mock sarcasm.

Watching Lawman's obvious pleasure with Dino's tactic, one could see the weight of countless pressures and frustrations, held silently for the past ten months, release themselves from Lawman's shoulders, as he honestly revealed, with a hearty laugh, "No, but I did see the face of Jesus!"

On the ramp

♦♦♦♦ I walk outside after the debrief and can't help but feel what a great day I've experienced. The weather was great, the show went well, and even the Gs felt good, relatively. There is a feeling of leftover adrenaline after a flight like that, and it feels good. Walking slowly across the ramp on spent legs, I understand better why these men smile so much some days, and also why they are so exhausted at day's end. The jets are sitting neatly in a row, with no obstructions, warmed by the late September sun. This is the perfect time to get those pictures. I walk with camera in hand to the end of the line, towards the #7 jet....

THE SEVEN JET

129

Dino matches the movements of the others as they climb down from their jets at the end of the performance. He appears entirely too calm for what he has just been through.

BLUE ANGELS *A Portrait of Gold*

TOP
Atop the Burke-Lakefront tower, Heyjoe acts as safety observer during the Cleveland National Air Show.

BOTTOM
With the march-down, another show begins. The first Blue Angel teams just walked out to their planes and climbed in. Given the choice, today's teams would probably do the same.

THE SEVEN JET

Echelon formation.

TOP
Taxiing out
with Dino.

BOTTOM
Lawman's
view on takeoff,
just moments after
Boss has called
for the raising
of the landing gear.

THE SEVEN JET

TOP
As the wheels are tucked away, Dino starts his move beneath Lawman's afterburners, en route to the slot position. The noise is deafening; the minimal clearance, startling.

BOTTOM
The Diamond Aileron Roll, where all four planes roll independently. The identical position of the planes caught on film is remarkable, given the imprecise nature of four pilots initiating four separate maximum rate rolls on command.

134 | BLUE ANGELS *A Portrait of Gold*

The Tuck-Under Roll as seen from #4, on a wonderfully clear day in Cleveland.

TOP
The Diamond 360, seen from the rare view of opposite the crowd line. From this perspective, #4's offset to the right is evident. as is the massive wing overlap.

BOTTOM
Following the Delta Loop Break, six planes will reposition, and turn back towards show center, attempting to cross simultaneously. From Dino's jet, this is the scene at the cross. The wide angle lens does not do justice to the close proximity of the planes.

OVERLEAF
The Boss eases the formation out a bit as they reposition behind the crowd for the next maneuver, and Lawman is able to do some sight-seeing of downtown Cleveland.

161983

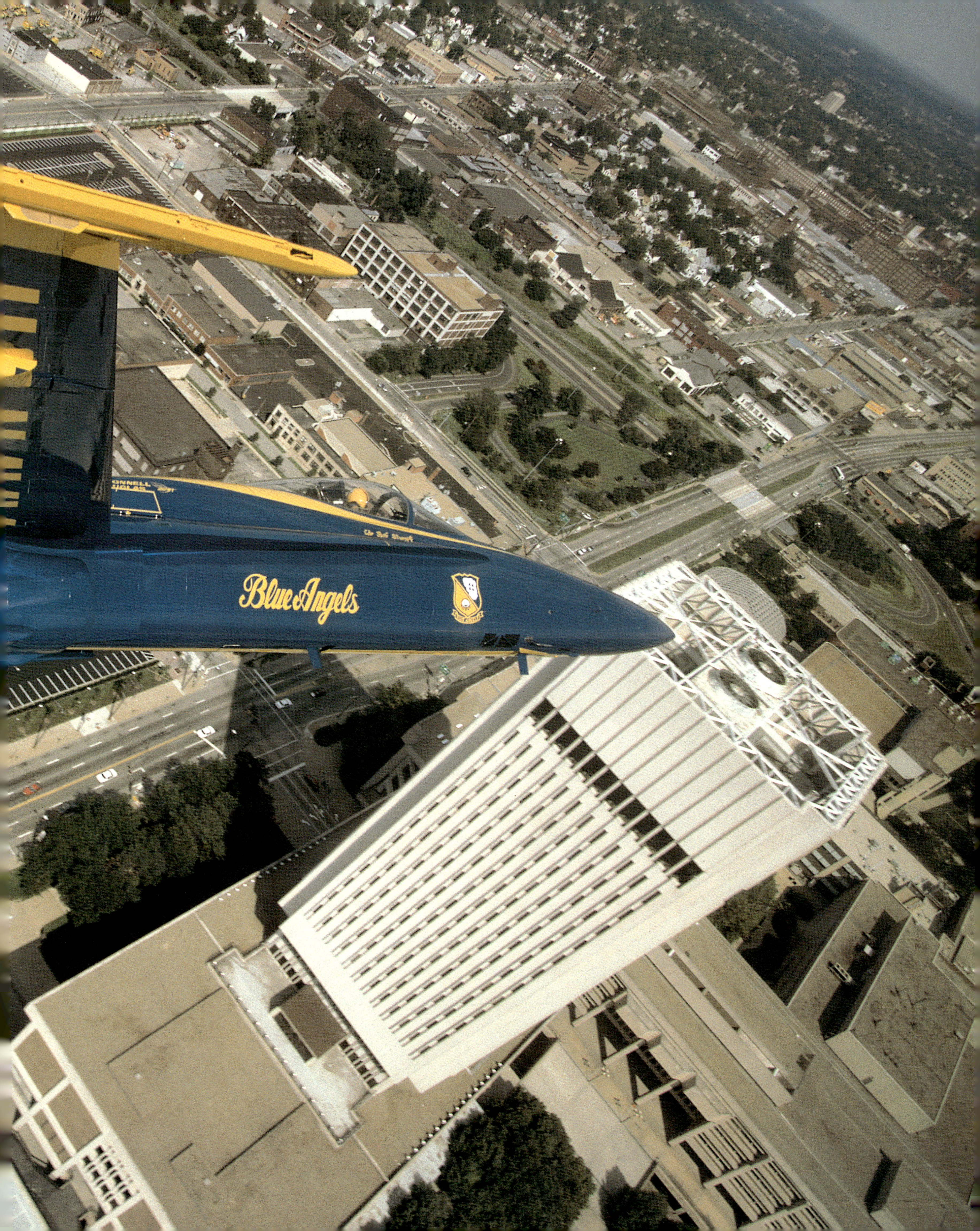
Blue Angels

138　　BLUE ANGELS *A Portrait of Gold*

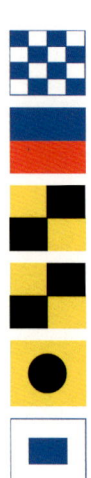

During the Exchange Day performances, each team took up a member of the other team. Lawman flew with Thunderbird #2, and Hoops took up the Air Force's lead solo – minus the G-suit.

8 Meeting of Giants

Nellis AFB, Nevada

♦♦♦♦ The Thunderbird ramp at Nellis has a unique look to it this weekend, as Blue Angel Hornets sit opposite Thunderbird F-16s. The occasion is called Air Exchange Day, and it won't be found on anyone's official list of air shows, but for the people in the local area, it will yield some of the best flying seen anywhere this season from America's two most prodigious aerial demonstration teams.

The Exchange Day affords both flying teams an opportunity to see how the "other side" does things. (The Army's Golden Knights Parachute Team also attends.) For some team members, it will be their first close-up look at how the other branch of service functions. The Thunderbirds and Blue Angels take turns hosting the event each year, and it has become an enjoyable meeting for both teams, offering a relaxing week of practice and a chance to compare notes with the only other guys in America who do what they do.

The true beneficiaries, however, are the local people invited out to the base to witness both teams flying back to back on Saturday morning. Though the day is not billed as such, this is a chance to see the two world giants of air show demonstrations go beak to beak in October, a time of the year when both teams are peaking in performance. Since the Blues and Thunderbirds will not be found on the same air show program anywhere, during the season, this is a rare opportunity to enjoy two renowned performers, and though the "show" is not officially advertised or open to the public at large, there isn't an empty seat anywhere.

For the military air show purist, who doesn't want to spend all day watching warm up acts, this is a no-nonsense line-up. The show consists simply of an opening jump by the Golden Knights, followed by Blue Angel and Thunderbird performances. By design, the Navy and Air Force demonstration teams will be the closing act at most of the shows they attend, meaning they will often have to fly through the unstable air of late summer afternoons. Conditions could not have been better for both teams at Nellis; the flights are scheduled to start early in the day, at a time when most air shows would normally just be opening their gates to the public. The cool fall morning yields calm winds and smooth air. The sight of the twelve jets lined up on a quiet Nellis ramp sends an air of anticipation through a crowd that had begun arriving hours early.

Though this crowd measures smaller in number than those seen throughout the year, the flight performances rises to heights reserved for the teams' best. There is no shortage of pride on either team, and though everyone tries to downplay the show as any sort of contest, a friendly competitive spirit is evident. Regardless of the number of spectators, the audience that the Blues most wants to impress is simply the six other guys on the host team with whom they share a common bond, and vice versa. Had there only been those six guys in attendance, the performances would have been as stellar.

There is much camaraderie and sincere mutual respect, and of course the usual shop talk about the differences in the jets. The single engine Thunderbird F-16 Fighting Falcon is smaller and lighter than the Blue Angel F/A-18 Hornet, and is one of the most maneuverable aircraft in the world; the Hornet, however, packs more muscle with twin engines, and its larger dimensions not only afford a bigger payload in combat but also give the air show spectator a nice blend of size and sound. Both jets employ modern fly-by-wire technology, where flight control movement is computer controlled. Due to operational requirement differences, however, these systems are integrated into each plane differently. By simply trimming in the forces electrically on their side grip stick, Thunderbird pilots can achieve the heavy stick feel necessary for this type of flying. Blue Angel pilots must employ an artificial spring system, placed against a centrally positioned stick, in order to attain the same feel. The Thunderbirds are unable to perform the Dirty Roll on takeoff, since control gains in the F-16 Fighting Falcon are computer dampened when the landing gear is down, sharply decreasing the roll rate. The computer systems used in the F/A-18 Hornet, though, allow for full roll capability with the gear lowered, and the Dirty Roll is a fixture in the routines of Blue Angel solo pilots. Overall, the two are pretty tough machines, and the teams who fly them eye each other's mounts with great interest.

Many think that the Blue Angels and the Thunderbirds are basically the same, simply dressed in the different colors of their respective services. On the surface both teams are quite similar: both use six jets, fly a diamond formation, and employ two solos in their routine. Closer inspection, however, reveals a different picture. To make a comparison of the two, the analogy could be used of comparing an apple to an orange. With the exception of their color, they are quite similar on the surface; both are round, both are fruit, and both grow on trees. But when you bite into an orange, you know it is definitely not an apple, and vice versa. And so it is with these two air show teams, coming as they do, from the two different family trees of the Navy and Air Force.

The Blues are amazed at the immense amount of equipment and people the Thunderbirds have in support of their team, while the Thunderbirds shake their heads in wonder that the Blue Angels can do all that this business entails, with a minimum of men and material. The Thunderbirds have a more colorful paint scheme on their planes, but the Blues are proud to retain their tradition of basic blue, with minimal designs, as it is a link to the basic paint scheme of the Navy's earlier line fighters. The Thunderbirds will alternate between several different colors of flight suits for shows, but wear regular Air Force issue flight suits when practicing and training. The Blues have just one color of flight suit, authorized for wear the entire time they are on the team, whether at practice or a show.

The Thunderbirds wouldn't dream that the team Flight Surgeon could help critique the pilots in flight as the Blues have him do. The Blues couldn't imagine a debriefing directed solely by the Leader, instead of the #4 pilot. G-suits, oxygen masks, show music – the list of differences goes on, but it is in the area where they are most similar, putting jets together in close formation, that they are the most difficult to compare.

The diamond formations flown by both teams are structured quite differently. The Thunderbirds fly slightly higher on the wing, and correspondingly, #4 is closer to the jet wash of the Leader. (This is why Thunderbird #4 always had a black tail during the team's F-100 and F-4 eras.) The Blue Angels fly a lower wing position, and #4 is positioned below the jet wash of #1; however, the Blues fly with more wing overlap – and coupled with the deeper stack, they can achieve a tighter formation. Although they incorporate similar formations, the two employ many different variations which have become trademarks of each team over the years. No one else does the Diamond Dirty Loop as do the Blue Angels, and no Thunderbird performance would be complete without the solo pilot spiraling up through the traditional Bomb Burst maneuver. The differences and skills of each team are plentiful. As to comparisons of which team is better – some days you prefer an apple; some days you like an orange. American audiences are fortunate to have two teams of this caliber flying under the same flag.

Certainly both teams have achieved a level of proficiency that few could claim, and this proficiency is why everyone watched with such intensity when the teams delivered back to back performances. In essence, Exchange Day affords team members an opportunity to learn more, about the differences in Air Force and Navy methods of conducting business. And those differences, in turn, greatly affect each team's approach to their demonstration flying.

As interesting as watching both teams fly in succession was watching the teams watch each other. There was a mix of curiosity, awe, and scrutiny, and most evidently, respect.

MEETING OF GIANTS

141

TOP
Backlit by an early morning sun, Blue Angel solos clear the Nellis mountains and head for show center. Their undisturbed smoke pattern indicates calm winds and smooth air.

BOTTOM
No competition, guys, just a friendly exchange of ideas, really. Yeah, right.

142   BLUE ANGELS *A Portrait of Gold*

The absolute bottom of the food chain.

Thunderbird Ramp

✦✦✦✦ I thought the Blues' best performance this year had been their show on the final day at Miramar. They seemed to really rise to the occasion there. But they did the same today, at the home of the Thunderbirds, and flew the best performance they would fly all season. Something about peer pressure which stirs these folks. The formations were tight, the solos were on the mark, and even the difficult six plane cross was magnificent. When they were through, they took their place on the ramp to watch "the other guys." The Blues were quiet, but I could tell they felt good about their performance. This was the first time all year I actually got the Boss to admit that they really had flown a good one. I knew then that it must have been as good as I thought, since rarely did this team ever admit to such. The Thunderbirds flew well also, and as far as who was best today, well, I'd hate to live on the difference. Regardless of any comparisons, the Blues felt good knowing they had done their best during the most unique of "shows" this season. Witnessing this level of performance in October was a testament to the months of flying together the Blues had now accumulated. Slowly, and painstakingly, they had reached a level of confidence and performance that could only come after much time invested.

Salinas, California

✦✦✦✦ The California International Air Show has grown greatly in size since its humble beginnings, and with the Blue Angels headlining this year's show, a record crowd for the event is reached.

There is a definite difference in the team's general mood from what I first observed earlier in the year. Over the many hours they've spent together, they've become more relaxed and comfortable with each other. There are still the thorough debrief sessions, but underlying them is a pervasive feeling that these men are truly enjoying the experience more. Even Lawman, who will be the new guy in the diamond all year, doesn't feel like a new guy anymore, and has shown the kind of progress that will carry him strongly into next season.

He is not there yet, though, and still must endure the close scrutiny the diamond demands. After a flight at Salinas, I complimented Lawman on how good his performance had looked from the ground. Quickly, he pointed out his displeasure over erring slightly on a maneuver which normally gives him little trouble. I assured him that none of the thousands of people in the crowd noticed so subtle a miscue, and not to worry about it. Walking with me across the ramp, Lawman smiled, put his hand on my shoulder, and said in an instructive tone of voice, "But Brian, my son, the three people who matter most did see it, and now Dino is going to have my butt in debrief." Then Lawman laughed in a way that told me he no longer dreaded such sessions as he once had. For him, like most of the pilots, the shows were not measured in crowd attendance or amounts of public praise, but rather in the amount of highlighting one might receive in the debrief.

Near the end of his first year though, Lawman had come to realize one of the fundamentals of Blue Angel flying. Simply stated, the flying never gets easier; it is always hard. But in time, you see more, and realize more precisely what you did in each maneuver, and eventually can enjoy the process more. The learning never ceases. This realization usually occurs late in the first season of a Blue Angel pilot, and better prepares him for his second winter training season, where others will then look to him for guidance.

More than just the formation of airplanes in the sky, the essence of the Blue Angel experience is about people – the people who make up the team, and the millions who are touched by their performances throughout the year. I saw the joy that this team can bring, in the faces of countless air show spectators across the country. I also saw genuine joy in the faces of team members when in the course of their travels, acquaintances with old friends were renewed. One of the most impressive aspects of the Blue Angel experience was to observe the sincere and personal attention given to special friends of the team. These friendships began in a variety of ways, each holding some special significance to the team. Each succeeding team embraces these friendships as their own, and ensures that the special relationship is continued. One example of this personal side to the team, often unobserved by the public, was witnessed at Salinas.

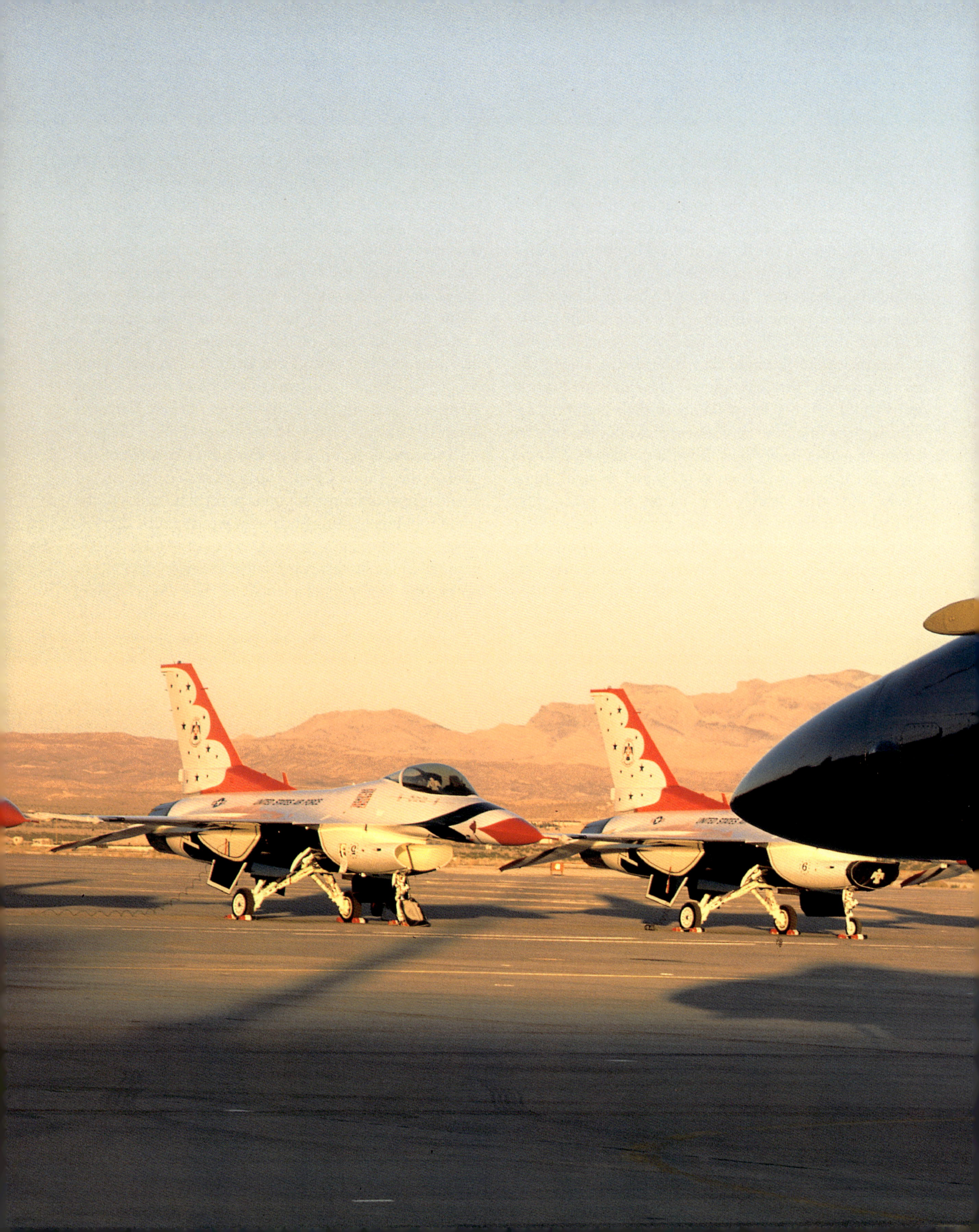

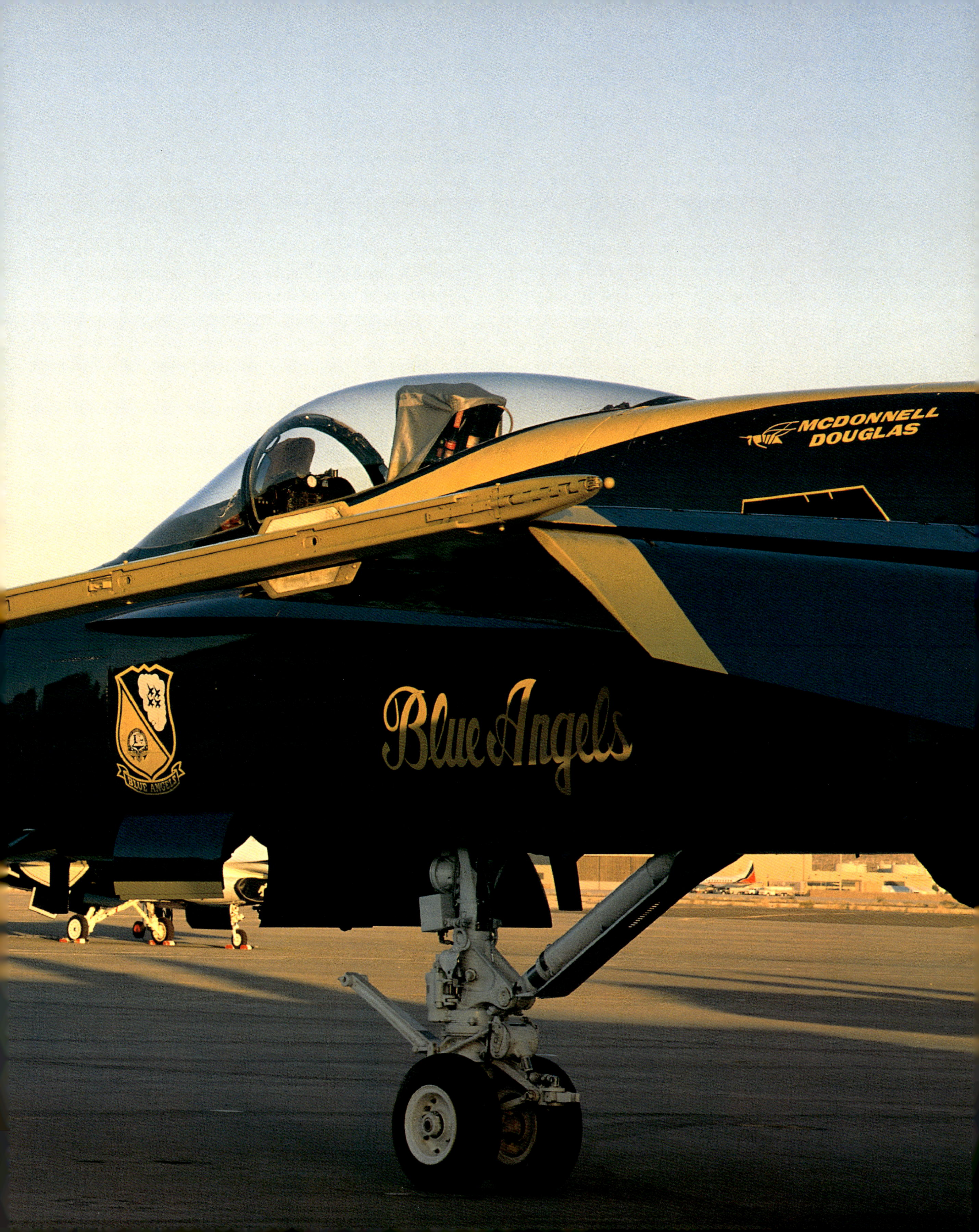
MCDONNELL
DOUGLAS
Blue Angels
BLUE ANGELS

Briefing with Donnie

♦♦♦♦ Several guests have been invited to attend the informal portion of the briefing. There are a couple of Navy pilots, one a former flight instructor of Dino's, and the other the Boss' first skipper. There was also one civilian, a man named Donnie. Donnie is an older man, and moves about slowly, but speaks with the wit and enthusiasm of one of the young pilots. This man intrigued me, and I learned that previously he had been a senior captain, instructor, and Chief Pilot for American Airlines.

As everyone sat around the room talking, the Boss looked up with a smile, and as if performing a team ritual, asked Donnie if he would be so kind as to share with the team any new jokes he had heard. From the mock grumblings and pseudo-insults of the pilots, I could tell that Donnie was held in high esteem with this group. Unfazed, Donnie slowly walked over to a chair and sat at the opposite end of the table from Boss. As Donnie began, in his George Burns style, one-liners flew from his mouth as a warm-up for his big joke finale. As the pilots listened and laughed, I knew there must be a story behind this former airline captain who so easily commanded the attention of the team.

I later learned that many seasons ago, Donnie had assisted several former Blue Angels through their application process with the airlines. They greatly appreciated his help and invited him as a guest of the team to view a Blue Angel performance. Donnie knew of the team, but had never really watched a complete show, especially from a front row seat. As a highly experienced aviator, he appreciated the show in all its subtleties and was moved by the performance.

Donnie wrote a letter of appreciation to the Blue Angels, thanking them for his special seat at the show. He also thanked the team for representing all that he had thought was truly special about aviation and pilots everywhere. The simple sincerity of this letter, written by a man so highly esteemed in the flying community, touched the team professionally, and he became a respected friend.

Shortly thereafter, Donnie suffered severe injuries when the limousine in which he was riding as a passenger was hit head-on. Eventually released from the hospital, Donnie's injuries left him with partial paralysis on one side of his body, and his flying days were over. Medically retired, he slipped into a life of quiet boredom and depression.

Surprised that the Blue Angels, now comprised of new members, were even thinking of him, he received a call from the team inviting him to their show as their special guest. With some assistance, Donnie showed up and tried to thank the team for their kindness, but found few words to express what he was feeling. When the team Narrator announced over the loud speaker that the show was being dedicated to their dear friend, Donnie, he was emotionally overwhelmed and, in his words, "cried right through the Double Farvel."

To a man who had spent much of life setting his personal feelings aside, the team had restored hope. Through their performance, they had brought him back to a place where a wounded spirit could take wing and still soar with the best. Of the thousands who viewed the Blue Angel performance that day, at least one man found renewed strength to rebuild the formation of his life, and now admits, "that simple show was a turning point in my life."

Donnie got stronger, regained his infamous sense of humor, and in time, was made an honorary Blue Angel, a title bestowed on only a few over the years. At the informal ceremony, Donnie gallantly held back tears of pride and said, "Somebody better tell a joke quick or I'm gonna start bawlin'." Since then, Donnie meets the team two or three times a year, whenever they are flying nearby. It is a tradition that Donnie starts off the briefing with some of his latest jokes.

♦♦♦♦ Most of the men in the room today do not know the entire story of how Donnie became an honorary Blue Angel, but honor him accordingly, and enjoy laughing at how horribly bad his jokes are. No one tells bad jokes as well as Donnie, and the briefing won't start unless he tells a few.

Amidst much laughter, and a respectful "Thanks Donnie" from the Boss, the guests left and another briefing began. On the way out, I asked Donnie where he had learned to fly. With a sparkle in his eye, he replied, "I'm still learning."

Hospitality Hangar

Frequently, the team will attend a reception in their honor following that day's show. Sometimes these are more informal gatherings of air show performers, and they offer a chance for the flyers and friends to eat and unwind after the day's events. Many times, people don't understand why Blue Angel pilots are often latecomers to these events. The reason, of course, is the team's strict adherence to thoroughly debriefing their performance following the show, regardless of how nice it might be to go directly to the hospitality tent, unwind with other air show folks, and debrief later.

Talking with the pilots, once they finally do show up, I am surprised that, at this point in the season, the debriefings are still nearly as long as earlier in the year. Dino points out that as the team gets better, the debriefs get more nit-picky to correct the smallest of errors. This is critical, since with greater proficiency comes a tendency to fly the jets even closer together, necessitating even more precise and thorough debriefs of every movement. As the pilots get better and more comfortable in their positions, Dino must also ensure the team does not get complacent, as this can be just as dangerous as early season roughness. "I can tell when this is happening," says Dino. "Usually about this time of the year, the wingmen are getting comfortable and start collapsing in a little on Boss. They forget sometimes that back in the slot, that means looking at a hundred thousand pounds of blue jets in my lap, so later in the year, I am more frequently telling them to move it out a bit." From winter to fall, the formation evolves, and only through the fine tuning daily by its members, does it survive.

By this time of the year, the new team members have been selected for next year's team, and accompany the Blues to the shows. The new Doc, Narrator, and a solo pilot join the team at the hospitality tent. Wearing their khaki uniforms, they of course stand out and are cut no slack by those they seek to join. Timber decides that it's "nice having the new guys here. Now at least there is something lower than Cubby on the food chain."

The continuous travel all year is starting to show in the fatigue of the pilots. More frequently, they will simply retire to their rooms for a good night's sleep. By October, team members have seen enough hotels, baggage, and rental cars. They never get to see enough of their families, and know that even though the season is almost over, there will only be a short break before they are gone again for nearly three months at winter training. Often, on the road, they will be unaware of the date, or even their next location, as the memory of a long season of travel starts to blur. Always they have each other though, and in the cohesion that is their team, they have a "family" on the road. They kid each other mercilessly, but are protective of the team from outsiders, especially those who misunderstand the team and might even want to malign its image.

With all its functional autonomy, though, this team does not get away with much. Every single complaint to the FAA or the Navy about the Blue Angels, regardless of how inaccurate or bizarre, must be answered by the team in writing. For all the acclaim the team receives throughout the year, there are still people who feel it's necessary to write their Congressman about the excessive jet noise over their community one weekend out of the year. They are all answered, politely and accurately, and because the Blue Angels follow air show guidelines professionally, they rarely need to respond twice.

♦♦♦♦ Standing with small plates of food, I notice the pilots besieged with questions from the many air show guests who want to speak with them. Tired now, not only from the day's events, but from a complete summer of travel, the team politely answers questions they've heard many times before and seem to genuinely enjoy interacting with the local folks. Sometimes, people want to simply tell the team how wonderful they think the Blue Angels are.

One eccentric, elderly woman captured the attention of several Blues as she described to them, with religious fervor, what a spiritual experience it was for her while worshiping God, as she heard the Blue Angels fly right over her church. "I felt as if Jesus was talking to me, and I could see His face," she proclaimed.

As she hurried off, Snooze and Dino just stared. Dino finally turned to Snooze and deadpanned, "I see the face of Jesus every day." Then that grin.

148   **BLUE ANGELS** *A Portrait of Gold*

Donnie spins a yarn for the boys prior to the briefing, and they love it. On the table sit cookies worth up to $5 apiece.

Timber at the initiation of his opening climb. Large deflection of horizontal tail reveals heavy aft stick. The crowd at Salinas followed his every move as he climbed skyward.

A couple of big guys. So what did the lead solo pilots of two of the world's premier flying teams discuss when they met? The number of daughters each had.

MEETING OF GIANTS

The Blues locked into a solid echelon formation.

OVERLEAF The Blues flew a solid show. The Double Farvel sparkled in the cool morning air.

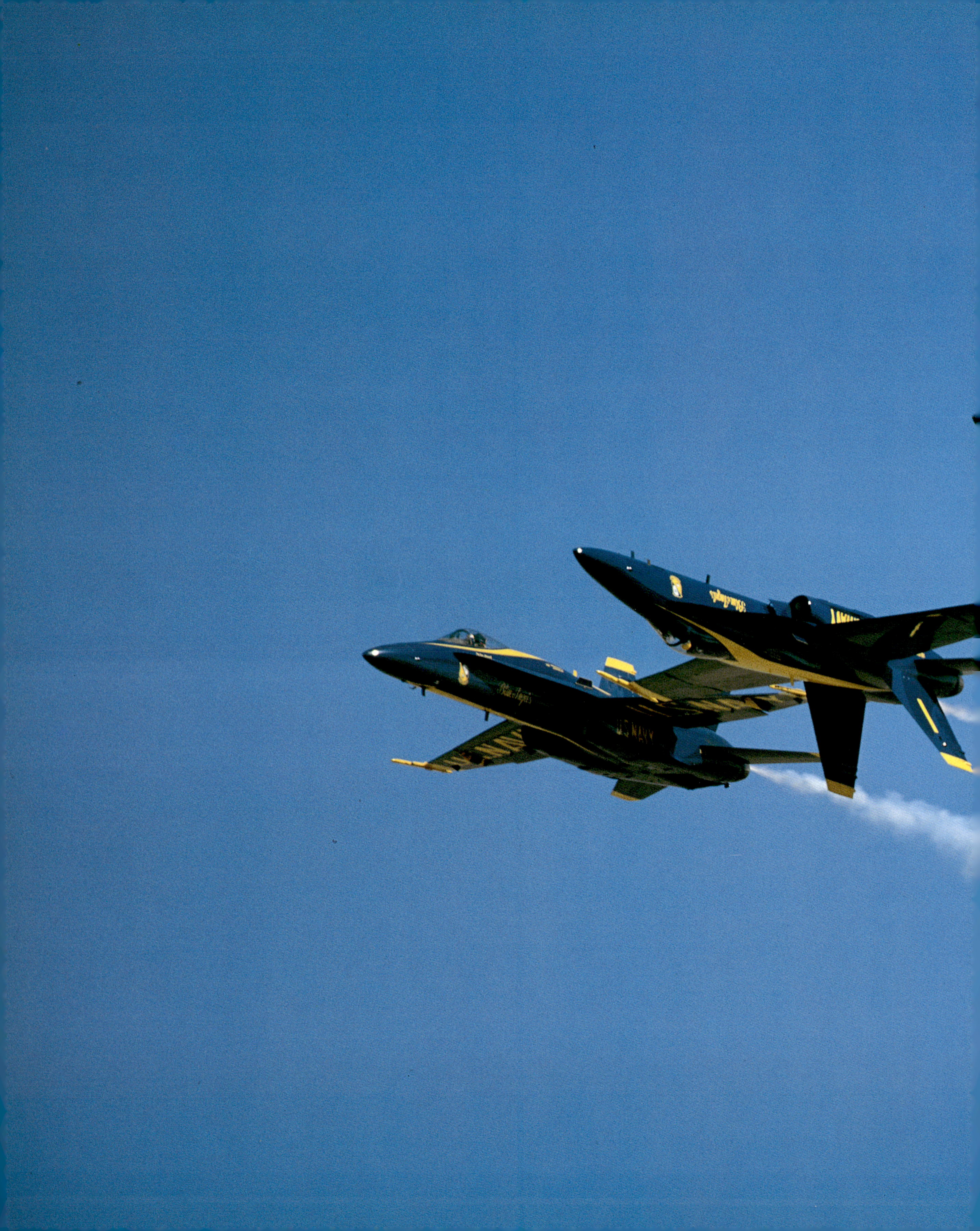

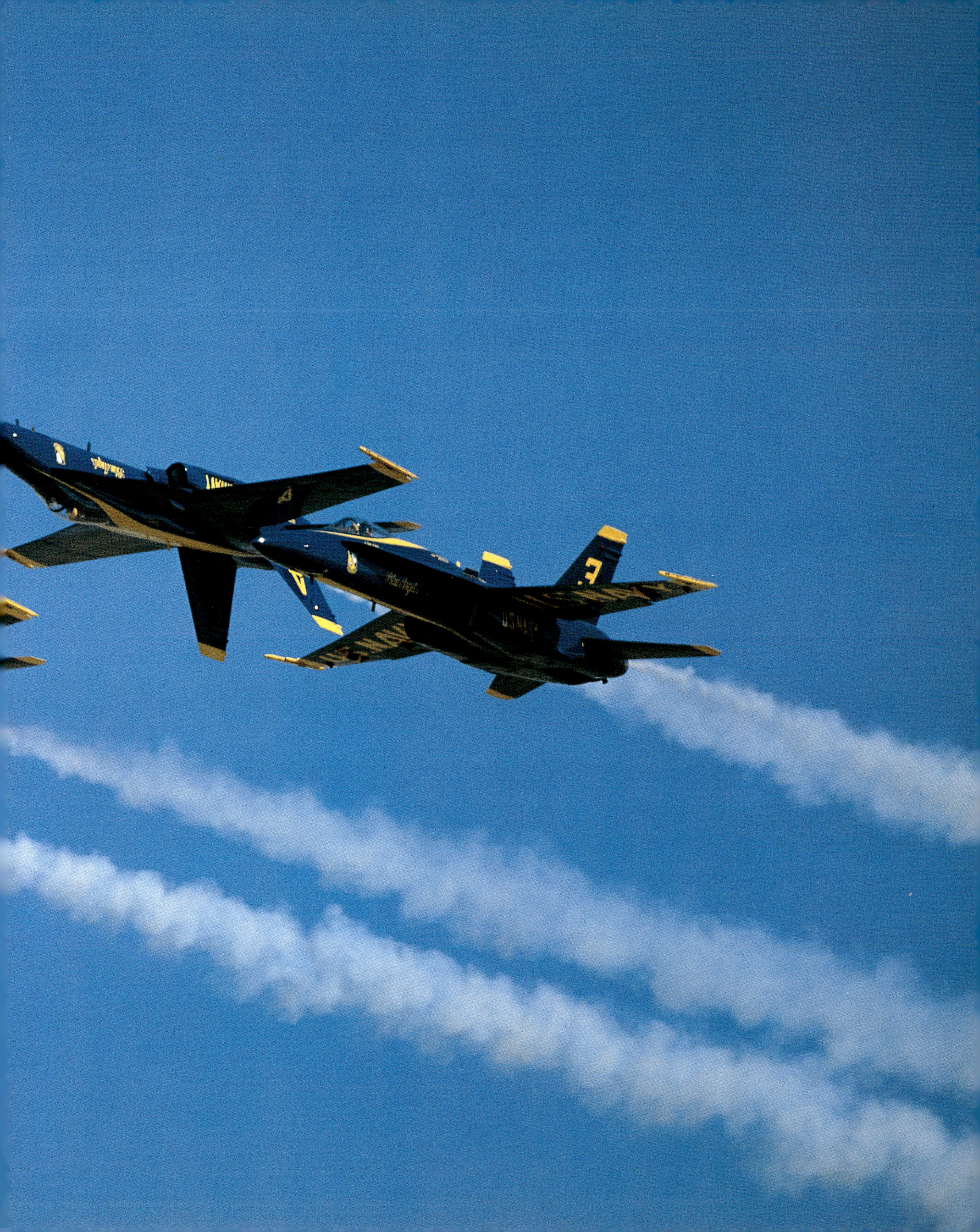

154 | BLUE ANGELS *A Portrait of Gold*

Hoops pushes out in the climb at -2.5Gs.

9 Autumn Gold

NAS Memphis, Tennessee

As the season winds down, the team seems like a completely different group than it was back in March. In a sense, they are, as they have evolved into a team whose confidence and proficiency didn't exist then. Sadly, the high level of performance the team has finally reached, will be all too short-lived. In reflecting about this, Snooze points out, "It takes us until about July or August to really start getting comfortable. Then around September, you actually start seeing your mistakes. That doesn't mean you can correct them always, but at least now you know exactly what is occurring. Then in October, you really start to enjoy it as everyone has really come together. But only for a few weeks, because then the season's over and this team is done, and we start all over again forming a new one at winter training."

Commits

✦✦✦✦ This morning there are a host of commits scheduled as usual. The Doc is going to St. Jude's Children's Hospital for a visit. Lawman is talking at an elementary school. The Fat Albert guys are speaking at a trade school. Just as winter training is the big equalizer in keeping everyone humble about their skills, the commits seem to be the equalizer during show season in keeping everyone "up." No matter how exhausting or frustrating the previous day was, team members are enthused and recharged by speaking to and visiting with the young people of a community. This is probably the most serious role one can have as a Blue Angel, and seems to be one of the most enjoyable for the team.

At St. Jude's, Doc visits several different wards, talking mostly with children who have very little chance of recovering from their illnesses. He speaks with the children as long as they want. For kids confined to the stale routine of hospital life, Doc's very presence is cause for excitement. He shows them pictures of the team and leaves Blue Angel handouts for them to read. Sometimes he doesn't talk about the Blue Angels, or the Navy, or anything remotely related to his line of work, but rather, talks with them about life in general and a host of topics that a young child can cover when he thinks someone is interested. Doc's visit is far removed from the usual recruiting trip that many commits represent. In his words, "If we can just brighten up the day of one child, then that is reason enough for being there."

In the hospital lobby, Doc is stopped by several staff members and parents of patients, all seeking a signature from one of the Blue Angels. They are surprised to see him there, but all are appreciative of his visit.

Most of the kids Doc speaks with will never play outside, or attend an air show, or ever see the Blue Angels fly. But for a few moments he brings a smile to their young faces and touches a part of the only life they will know.

Across town the Marines are addressing a group of young folks who have had problems in public schools with drugs or gangs, and are getting a second chance through a special school. After showing a video on the Blues (highlighting Fat Albert of course), Wilbur and Heyjoe field questions and offer some good advice to an audience whose attention they have. The kids are surprised to hear that Marines are part of the Navy Blue Angels. Wilbur admonishes the kids who prefer gangs to learning. He tells them if they want to belong to a group so badly, come join the Marines, a pretty tough "gang" in its own right and an organization that can teach you something too. The kids smile at the comparison of the Marines to a gang, and they listen, and they think about the bold words these men in uniform are saying.

NAS Memphis Flightline

▼▼▼▼ I watch the solo pilots doing their arrival maneuvers. Locating precise geographical references is critical to their timing, and they make several passes around the edges of the field. Getting two jets, speeding toward each other at 800 knots of closure, to arrive at show center together takes timing, some luck, and lots of practice.

Life for the solos is a radically different experience than for the diamond pilots. The diamond lives in a world of inches, and sometimes sheer terror. The solos work in the realm of seconds, and half seconds, and also some moments of sheer terror, and many moments of sheer pain. The pain is relative, of course, to solo pilots who are used to doing it daily, but no one on the team climbs out of their jet more spent after a performance.

Nowhere in the Blue Angel routine is the absence of the G-suit more noticeable than when flying with the solos. Taking the jet to the limits of maximum performance, their routine will traverse from -2.5G to +7.5G. These are limits pushed only by the strong, and rarely is this type of flying called fun. Besides the heavy G forces sustained are the maximum rate rolls, accomplished many times throughout the performance. After flying with #5, one Blue Angel enlisted man said, "If you don't black out, then you'll probably puke from the rolls. By the time we hit the inverted stuff, I had done both." Snooze, who is built like an Abrams tank, said he has no desire to fly with the solos, even when they've offered to take him up. Cubby has done it, and measures his success on solo flights with how full, or empty, his air sickness bag is when through.

While most good fighter pilots could handle the stress of the routine, none would be able to perform it as precisely as the Blues' solos without a serious amount of practice. Hoops and Timber are not just good – they are driven, and must be, to deliver a maximum performance routine while wrestling forces fighting against them.

▼▼▼▼ Watching them practice a Tuck-Away Cross, I note how close the trailing jet passes to the other's jet wash. The McDonnell Douglas engine rep, also watching from the comm trailer, explains why this maneuver gives him a headache even though he doesn't fly it: "The trailing jet crosses so close to the lead plane, that its engine gets an immediate gulp of hot exhaust, causing the inlet temperature probe to go crazy. This is about the only time we get some occasional engine fluctuations on these otherwise very reliable engines."

I recall Timber's words about the solo maneuvers being more fluid than simply precise. While the diamond relies on some very specific references on the aircraft to hold a defined position, many of the tasks required of the solos during a show require estimations. Not only will they be solving rendezvous problems with the diamond (Line-Abreast Loop and Delta sequence), but also among themselves for their tandem maneuvers.

The solos must reposition constantly during a show, timing their entry and exit from show center to deconflict with the diamond. Due to the fluid nature of some of their maneuvers, no two ever flown are quite the same. Like the diamond, the solos are constantly reevaluating themselves and learning the subtleties of their routine throughout the entire season.

Due to the nature of the solo performance, geographical references and especially hazardous obstructions require a thorough inspection during these pre-show flights. Running in at 200 feet inverted is no time to first discover that the ground insidiously rises throughout the approach. #5 and #6 beat the field up until they must land to refuel. Throughout the solos' orientation, Doc and Mo talk to the pilots from the comm trailer, offering assessments of how close to show center their "hits" were occurring.

▼▼▼▼ After landing, Hoops confers with Mo about a problem he is having with his jet, and wants to know if it can be fixed before tomorrow's show. There is a practice flight scheduled for later today and Mo says, "Give me your jet this afternoon, and I'll have it ready for you by tomorrow." The #7 jet is readied and Hoops tells me to get my helmet. Flights with the solos are rare, and I move quickly.

With the Solo

♦♦♦♦ Every strap that was tightened while flying with the diamond is pulled twice as tight now. This is exciting flying, but it is not comfortable flying. The basic charter is given by the #5 crew chief after I'm securely attached to the seat with nine different connections. Smiling as if he knew something I didn't, he said, "OK, now, if you cry, faint, or throw up within the next forty minutes, they aren't going to stop the show. If you die, they'll probably skip the Delta maneuvers since they don't like those anyway. Good luck, sir." By this point in the season I'd gotten stronger, so I figured I probably wouldn't die, and if I cried, fainted, or threw up, I would kill myself anyway. (Something about peer pressure, here.)

The first thing evident about flying with the solos is that nothing is done gently. Every control is slammed, pulled, or pushed hard, and so is one's body. Those 270 degree solo exit rolls, from the ground, look fairly benign, but in the cockpit become a violent head-snapping whirl of earth spinning about the canopy. Anticipation is the key. Now, however, there is no "Hang on" issued from the front seat. There is no time, and Hoops is concentrating too much on not hitting the ground or Timber, to worry about that. Instead, I listen for his call to #6 of "Reeaaaddyy HIT IT!" and know that some violence will be done to our jet at that point. This call initiates their rolls or turns to help synchronize them.

The problem I experienced with the diamond pilots hitting my knee with the stick was intensified with Hoops. Very few times in the diamond routine does the pilot need to push the stick full left or right forcefully. For the solos it is a way of life, and my knee is battered by the metal hood of a stick housing a variety of weapons switches. Just minutes into the routine, I am glad that all my straps had been tightened beyond normal.

Setting up for the Tuck-Away Cross, I begin to see how far from the actual air show environment the solos fly at times to set up for their next maneuver. Coming toward the crowd line, I am surprised at how close we were to Timber, considering what I knew would happen next. As Timber approaches the runway with a "Rreeeaaddyy HIT IT!" Hoops slams us into a hard 270 degree roll opposite #6, throwing our jet forcefully through Timber's exhaust. With a loud thump, similar to a motorboat hitting a wave at high speed, we bounce through the hot wake of Timber's jet. I knew the temperature probe was probably getting a workout at that point, and so was I. My entire body flexes in an effort to withstand the immediate onset of 7Gs, as I fight to retain clear vision throughout the turn away from show center. Just about the time things start to feel normal, Hoops snaps us through one of those exit rolls. As we set up for our next entry, I am already drenched with sweat and it is still early in the routine. My fingers have gone numb from clenching the hand grips on each side of the cockpit.

Watching from the comm trailer, the jets at 200 feet don't seem so close to the ground. From the cockpit, flying inverted at 200 feet makes the trees look like they are in our lap. The roll to inverted is crisp and Hoops stops the roll aggressively, with wings level. Looking up at a runway speeding over the top of our canopy, I am reminded of being in the double Farvel, except this is lower. Aside from the blood being pushed toward my head from the -1G required to hold level inverted flight, the inverted passes are more total concentration than discomfort. Watching Timber's jet approach us inverted is a unique sight, as he appears right side up to us, but the runway and sky seem misplaced. Above his canopy, the "sky" had now become a ribbon of concrete runway, as we flew "above" a void of blue space. Flying inverted head-on to another jet in a like attitude is not something one witnesses often, even after many years of flying fighters. I find this to be an exhilarating experience and within a few passes, it begins to look normal.

Not so normal, is enduring the -2G push out, as Hoops climbs away from show center inverted. This is followed rapidly with a roll and pull to near 7G's. The human body is hard pressed to keep up with this rapid transition through a wide range of G forces. Going from -2Gs to +7Gs within one second leaves my body feeling a little like a cocktail shaker that had mixed my blood thoroughly. We are truly riding on the edge of performance for both man and jet.

The large stopwatches in the cockpits are monitored by both pilots as they attempt to arrive at show center simultaneously. In the same manner that the Boss calls out cues over the radio for the diamond, Hoops and Timber exchange time and distance information as they speed toward each other, adjusting their airspeed to make it work. As Hoops estimates the closure rate of the blue Hornet coming toward us, he will time his "HIT IT" call accordingly. Watching this process of stopwatch, land references, and seconds to go, I can see that with all the precise control required to fly this way, the routine is still very much an imprecise art.

Instead of "workin' the bug," Timber tells us he is "workin' a little early," which denotes he is a half second ahead of his mark on the run-in. Timber only has seconds to adjust his speed to compensate, and with a blue blur abeam us, two jets cross within feet of show center.

One of the most exciting and difficult maneuvers that the solos fly is the Double Tuck-Over Roll. Flying close formation while inverted is another one of those rare experiences, and it is difficult to perform properly. Timing the 270 degree roll in unison is as challenging as anything the solos will do.

♦♦♦♦ Looking off our wing, inverted, I see Timber's jet, also inverted. In this configuration, his plane is now strangely covered in shadow across the entire top of his fuselage and wings, while sunlight brightly lights the bottom of his jet. Hoops cares little about the inverse lighting patterns, as he is concentrating hard on his lateral positioning, insuring clearance to complete the roll. We are at 180 feet, but in this type of formation, it feels like about 40. Hoops slams the stick left with the same force as when we are upright, and in a flash of four wings, both jets turn out from the runway in an echelon type of formation.

The solos now look to join the diamond to form the Delta formation. While en route to rejoin, Hoops switches off the inverted fuel boost pumps, puts his visor down, and loosens the torso harness so that "I won't have to fly on the wing with a curved spine." Once joined up, Hoops and Timber form the ends of the Delta and commence flying a formation radically different from everything they have been doing the past thirty minutes. Dino waves as Hoops arrives on the left side of the formation.

♦♦♦♦ Taxiing in after landing, Hoops and I are both feeling the effects of slight dehydration. I welcome the water at the van with an even greater craving than after diamond flights. As I watch Hoops dismount his aircraft, I now recognize him as a combatant who, after forty minutes, has wrestled the jet to a draw. I have seen this man prepare himself in the weight room, and I now understand his intensity. It is a contest every day for him, and his opponent never loses strength. And the dangers never lessen.

The slightest hesitation of movement in the routine can beat a solo pilot right into the ground. It can beat the solo when it is done right, too; but it will let him live. Hoops and Timber have learned to live on the edge by pushing their aircraft, and themselves, to maximum performance; and they thrive there, on the edge, in the world of the solo pilots.

Memphis Debriefing

♦♦♦♦ A small boy has lost his parents, and has made his way to the building where the team is debriefing. Cubby offers to sit with him until his folks can be located.

In the briefing room, the solos are taking some grief from Snooze: "They fly a long routine since they need all that warm-up for the Delta." Timber, without looking up, calmly states, "We fly our best formation when alone."

The lively team mood connotes two things: they are flying some of their best performances of the year, and they are almost done for the year. They have worked hard all season, and though now enjoying the fruits of their labors, they look forward to the rest that season's end brings. I look around the room at these men whom I've observed for many months, and feel like I know them well. I realize now that I had memorized their names at the beginning of the year for nothing, as I know them best now only by what they call each other.

Lawman is on the phone with one of the new pilots who has been selected for next year's team. His advice is to "spend plenty of time with your family, and get down to the gym and start working out NOW!"

Hoops kids hard with me in the debrief, and I know that is a sign that I "passed" my flight with the solos: "Nice having you along today, Brian – at least now there's someone older than Boss at the table." After Snooze chimes in with some remark about my Air Force T-shirt, I begin feeling like one of the guys. This feeling of complete acceptance by the team is only occurring now, near the end of the season, and it is a good feeling, similar to the badge of black and blue that I now wear on my left knee.

Cubby comes back into the room, saying that the little boy's parents should be here shortly. "That was really nice, what you did, Cubby," says Boss, "and thanks for taking care of that. Oh, and Cubby, five bucks for being late to the debrief."

I talk to Hoops about the solo routine, and he explains some of what he was looking at today. His final comment on solo flying is typical of these men, and could well apply to the team as a whole: "In this routine, you're only as good as the man next to you."

The team finishes its debriefing, and Cubby comes back in with the little boy, now with his parents. They simply want to thank the team for their concern and for Cubby's assistance to their son. Everyone signs the boy's hat, and he leaves one happy little dude.

This is a nice finish to one of the more enjoyable debriefs experienced all year. Now that it is time to leave, the Boss performs his final function of the day: " Oh, Cubby – that'll be an additional five for *interrupting* the debriefing."

BLUE ANGELS *A Portrait of Gold*

TOP
Tough guys, solos. Timber and Hoops complete the final portion of the march-down as the others have already peeled off for their jet.

BOTTOM
Blue Angel crew chiefs stand ready to begin show sequence.

OVERLEAF
Doc grades each maneuver while Mo controls the airspace at the comm trailer.

AUTUMN GOLD 161

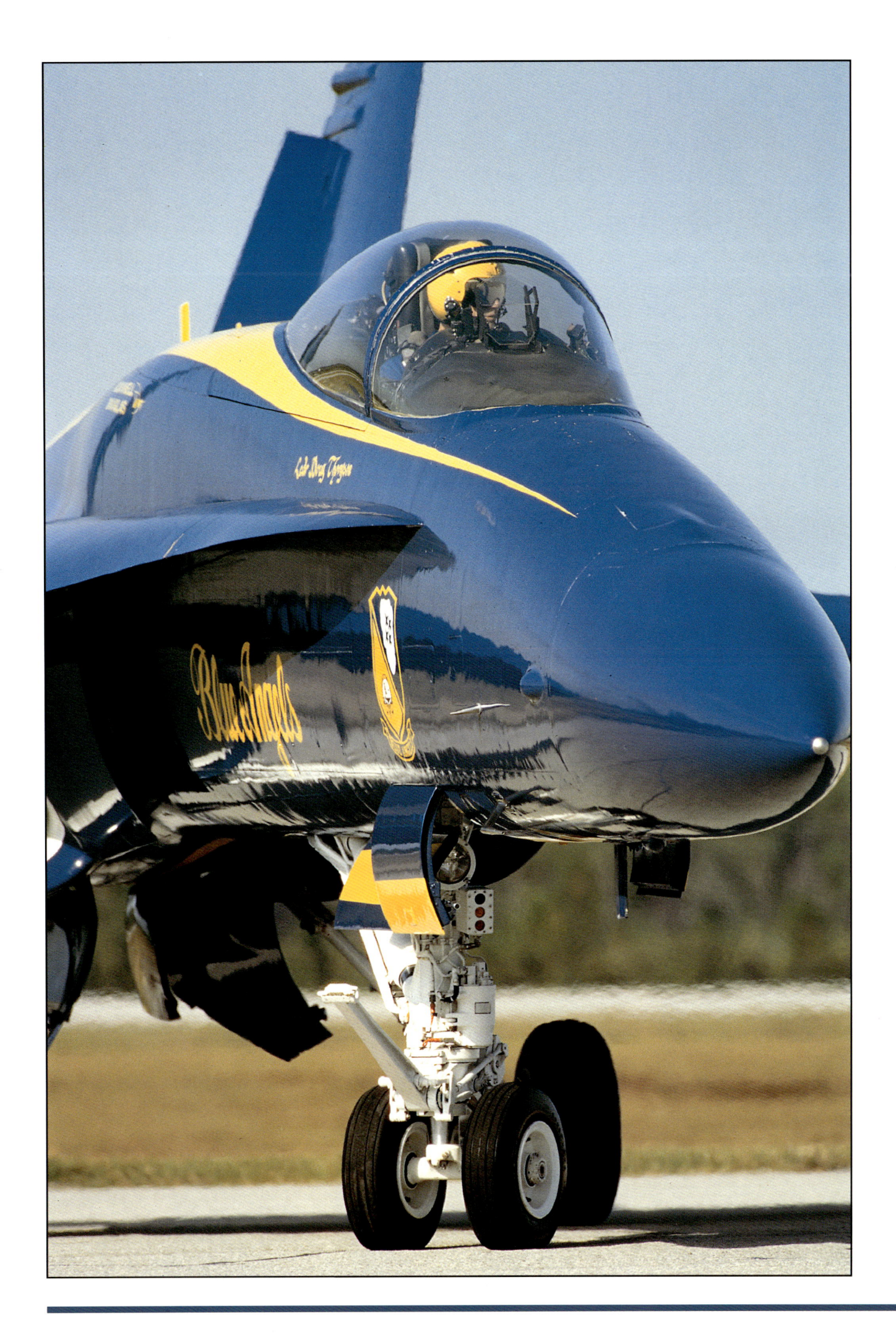

162 BLUE ANGELS *A Portrait of Gold*

Dino, Daddy, Hoops, and Surge fulfill autograph requests. When they finish, they will pose with special groups such as the Make-A-Wish-Foundation, an organization they actively support.

AUTUMN GOLD

163

Portrait of a Blue Angel solo.

164 BLUE ANGELS *A Portrait of Gold*

Nice hit.

AUTUMN GOLD

TOP
The Fortus maneuver, the solos' answer to the diamonds' Dirty Loop.

BOTTOM
Daddy need say nothing here, as the six jets crossing show center at NAS Memphis speak for themselves.

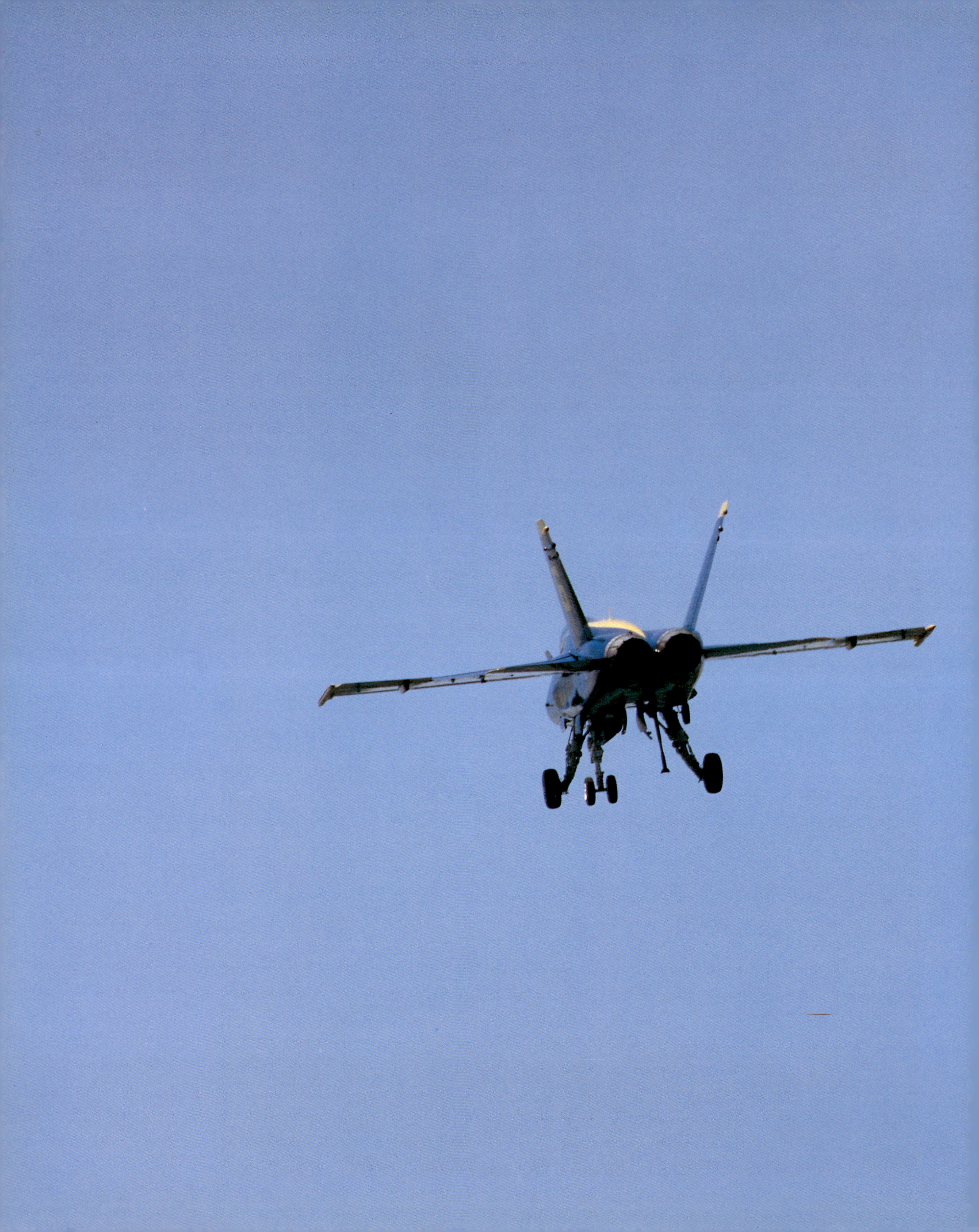

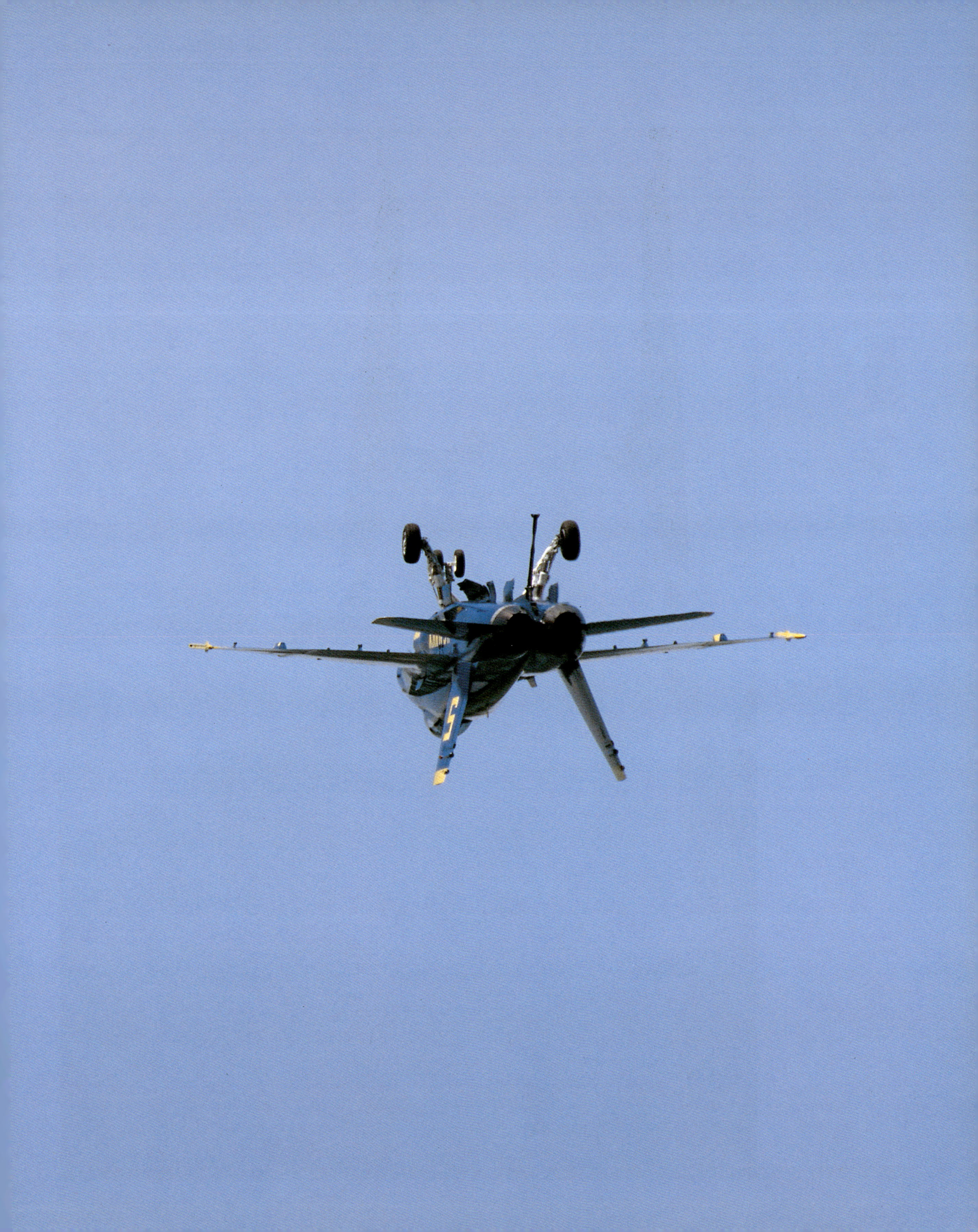

BLUE ANGELS *A Portrait of Gold*

10 Silent Passage

NAS Pensacola, Florida

The final Blue Angel show of the season is the Homecoming Show, flown in November at Pensacola Naval Air Station. It marks the end of a season that has extended well past the air show days of summer. For some, the show will mark their last performance as a Blue Angel, while those who will replace them gather and watch eagerly from the comm trailer. For the guys staying another year, it's business as usual.

The day before the final show, I stood on the Blue Angel ramp and waited for the team to land from their final practice. I noticed an elderly man talking with one of the McDonnell Douglas tech reps. He appears to be one of those special friends of the team as everyone seems to know him as simply "Grandfather." He once held the job of the man to whom he is speaking, and has a history with the team that few could match.

I found that Grandfather served as the Grumman representative to the Blue Angels during the team's halcyon days from 1951 to 1968. As the first company to provide planes to the Blue Angels, Grumman enjoyed a special relationship with the team that lasted over two decades, and Grandfather spearheaded that effort.

He went with the team on every trip, and loved helping the team out in any way he could. Besides his normal technical duties, he did everything from help with transportation, to give the team meal money in those early days. He was there in '65 when the team dazzled the audience at the Paris Air Show, and still shows a picture of the team over the Eiffel Tower as his most prized momento from those days.

Grandfather finally retired at the end of the Tiger jet era, after a distinguished career with Grumman. His days with the team are his most cherished memories, and he has a house full of more Blue Angel memorabilia than anyone alive today. Grandfather was solely responsible for preparing the Blue Angel archives for the Pensacola Air Museum, and is one of only eight men ever bestowed with the title Honorary Blue Angel Flight Leader.

Now 85 years old, he is a living part of Blue Angel history, and keeps close ties with the squadron. To this day, when new members come to the team each fall, it's Grandfather who takes it upon himself to get a list of their names from Cubby, and present them each with keys to the city of Pensacola. Watching current Blue Angels interact with Grandfather, I saw another example of how this team rich with tradition nurtures its present by honoring its past.

In the Squadron

✦✦✦✦ I catch Lawman in a reflective moment sitting at his desk, recounting his first year as a Blue Angel. I am curious if there were ever any times when he had truly enjoyed the experience. I am happy to hear him reply, "There were some times when it was all working perfectly, and you could get out of yourself for a moment and see this picture of beauty, with all the jets together – and then get jerked back to reality with the sound of Dino's voice screaming in your ear." Lawman laughs heartily, but adds that he would always remember the picture he had in his mind of the setting October sun hitting the gold lettering on the planes next to him as they flew over the Golden Gate Bridge.

Hoops, who had cleaned out his desk, says he is going to take a step back in technology from the Hornet and return to flying the F-14. Like Dino, who is returning to an F/A-18 unit, he is happy to be able to continue flying. The Boss would likely return to the fleet as a Commander in the Hornet, deploying back to "the boat." Once gone, these men would never don the Blue Angel crest again. Once they are done on this team, their time is over, and it's someone else's time.

Final Debrief

✦✦✦✦ Following the homecoming show, the team retires to the briefing room for the last time this season; only today, they have brought along their wives and families. This is the one performance of the year when there is no formal debriefing. Instead, the pilots get a chance to say their farewells, and make any last comments. Most are quick to thank their wives for their support throughout the year.

The Boss also thanks the team for all their support, and is proud to note that there was not one accident on his watch as Leader. Lawman says he looks forward to next season, and is "glad to be here." In a few days, Lawman will be checking out the new Boss, as he takes him through the flight profile. Snooze, who will begin his third year with the team in the slot, ends on a serious note, saving his next round of stories for next year's team. Dino tries gamely to bid farewell in his deep authoritative voice. But the tall man from Missouri, who had given three years of his life to this team, hits some unexpected turbulence of the throat and gets a little choked up. For a rare moment, #4 has less than complete control.

Following the festivities, the new team is introduced at dinner. At that moment, they are the Blue Angels, and the old team ceases to exist. The next day, signs in the parking lot are already changed, desks have been cleaned out, and the new team has taken over the squadron as if nothing had changed. Silently, new names have been added where appropriate, and the team goes on with squadron business as usual. In one week, the team will start flying the new guys in preparation for their January departure to El Centro.

Final Shutdown

✦✦✦✦ As the team lands for the final time before leaving for winter training, I watch the ritual of post-flight activities that I had witnessed so often in the past year. After climbing out of the jets, the pilots talk briefly with the crew chiefs and among themselves as always, while maintenance people quickly bed the jets down for the evening. Looking at the team now, I see them in a much different light from when I first witnessed their routine long ago. These are not show folks, just Navy professionals tending to business. The most heralded air show team in our nation's history, now seems far removed from the hype and mystique that accompanies its name. There is no hype, just maintainers and aviators working hard together to get a job done. The mystique I sought to uncover had slowly evaporated throughout a year of sweat, toil, and friendship, and left me observing just ordinary people, performing extraordinary tasks, while making them seem routine – nothing new from a Navy that does that on a daily basis around the globe. The Blues were simply honest representatives of the service that had trained them and sanctioned their public demonstrations. In my mind, I could picture the same scene before me, occuring on the deck of any one of our nation's carriers far out at sea.

Living around these people had changed my perspective of what the Blue Angel experience was all about. This was not a show party, but a show of continuous practice and performance. Where once I had seen maneuvers like the double Farvel as pure showmanship, I now saw them as more substance, representative of the flying skills of people who train to land on "the boat."

Any visions I had of meeting prodigy supermen of flight had vanished with the self-exposure of honest men with honest fears, and no false bravado – men willing to face the challenges and frustrations of striving together for perfection with imperfect skills. They put it all on the line, every day, and asked only for that opportunity.

Even the basic block numerals on the tails of the jets now appeared differently to me. Where once I had thought them to be too plain for an air show demonstration paint scheme, I now realized them to be representative of the same unpretentious style that was used on all Navy jets in the fleet; the substance over flash that Butch Voris had spoken of. In a single season, I had come to know a substance with this team that shone brighter than any paint scheme could.

As the pilots walked from the ramp, I knew I would view them, and those succeeding them, forever differently than I had. They were not men of mystique – just pilots who laughed often, shook hands a lot, loved to eat, and could fly, really fly. I knew we had created the mystique ourselves, we spectators who loved watching them, talking about them, and even writing about them. That the Blue Angels, through all that they do, can instill such pride and motivation in so many makes them worthy of our acclaim. And in that process, they ensure their flame of recognition will long be lit.

Leaving a quiet ramp, I understood the mystique surrounding this team better, now that its human character had been revealed to me.

Winter Training, El Centro, California

♦♦♦♦ Standing near the comm trailer, in the remote bleakness of the southern California desert, I watch the team go through their second practice of the day. Show season is not far off.

Mo has the radio speaker on, and it comes alive with the sound of Snooze's voice, critiquing the last formation:

"That has to stop NOW!... I don't EVER want to see that again.... Did you SEE that big blue thing next to you?..."

And so the tradition continues. Regular guys, workin' hard.

BLUE ANGELS *A Portrait of Gold*

SILENT PASSAGE | **173**

The flame is passed to the new #1 – Commander Donnie Cochran.

BLUE ANGELS *A Portrait of Gold*

TOP
Grandfather.

BOTTOM
The final handshake.

SILENT PASSAGE

*It' had been
a long season,
filled with good
memories from
traveling with
these men called
Blue Angels.*

*The Boss had never
smiled as brightly as
when his wife visited
at Miramar.*

*The lack of a
program was
no deterrent
to a youngster at
Traverse City
who handed
Lawman
an original drawing
of his jet to sign.*

*Snooze laughed on
the ramp at Luke
with anyone who
would listen.*

*During Family Day
at Pensacola,
Dino lost that
detached look
for a while,
and became
very attached
to his son.*

*Hoops talked to the
crowd at Redmond
with the same
intensity- and
finesse- he applied
in the cockpit.*

*Timber was sorry
at Cleveland that
Cubby wasn't along,
as kidding him
was getting to be
a part of his
pre-briefing ritual.*

*And somehow,
it was quickly over,
and a new Boss
arrived, and as fast
as new names
could be painted
on the jets, there was
a new team.*

BLUE ANGELS *A Portrait of Gold*

*ABOVE
Hoops slices through Timber's jet wash in the Tuck-Away Cross.*

*BELOW
Flying a flat show because of the low cloud cover, the solos overtake the diamond in a maneuver seldom seen.*

TOP
Prior to the pull up into the Dirty Loop, Dino sets his position securely.

BOTTOM
Stormy weather cancelled a practice show near end of season.

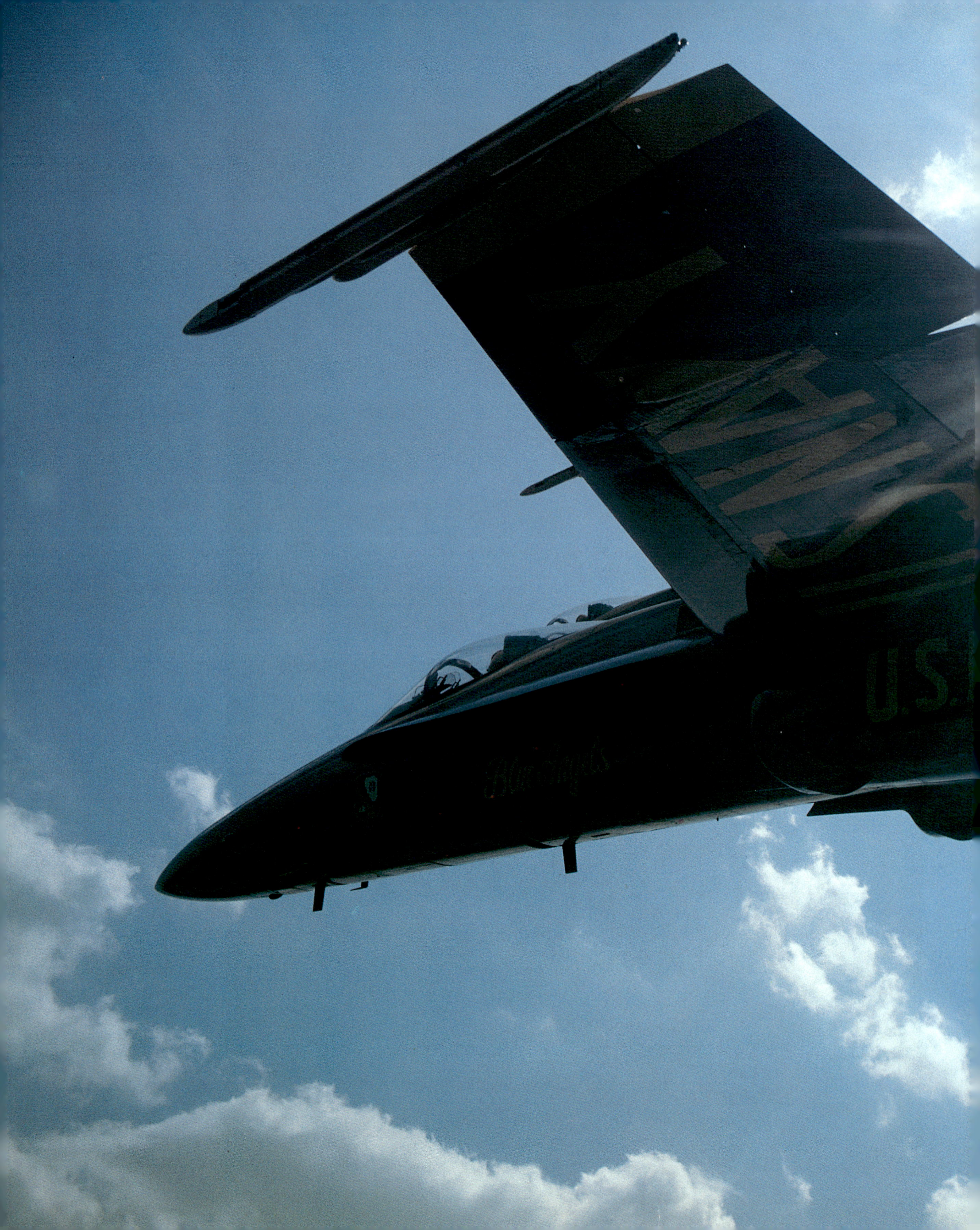
U.S.

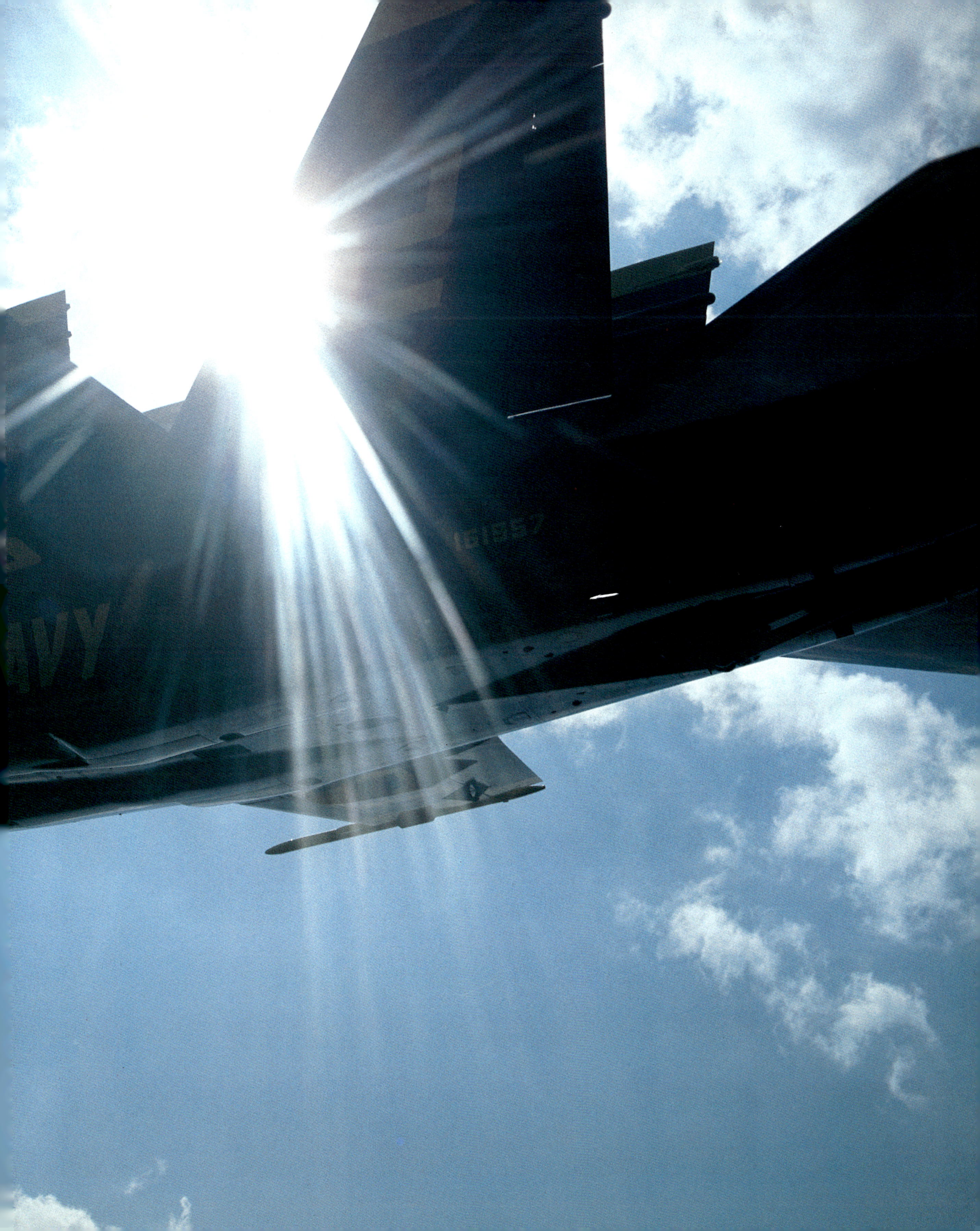

Above the desert of El Centro, a new team takes shape.

Epilogue

I first saw the Blue Angels fly when I was a boy of ten. Few things in my young life left such an indelible impression as those captivating blue jets that pierced the sky, along with my imagination, on that memorable day. Following the team throughout the years, I, like so many others, became a fan of those brash Navy flyers. Somewhere during an Air Force career, I envisioned doing a book like this, though I knew that many things would have to fall into place for it to become a reality. Luckily for me they did.

Most important was the approval given to my project by the 1994 Blue Angels themselves. Only with their willing assistance and cooperation could this book have been created. My sincere thanks to every member of that team for the special opportunities afforded me during a most unforgettable year.

Trying to capture the essence of the Blue Angel experience in the confines of a book would depend, in part, on the photographs I could obtain. I concentrated on trying to photograph the Blue Angels in ways that would show people a view of the team they would normally never see.

Throughout the year, whenever my camera was in hand, safety was always my first concern. This was particularly important while in the air. I ignored many picture taking opportunities while in the cockpit, due to my constant awareness of a stick moving between my knees. I kept equipment to a minimum, did not mount any cameras for self-portraits, and learned to change film in ways I never thought possible. The pilots were trusting me to handle my equipment, and myself, appropriately in the cockpit – a trust I did not take lightly. Many times, this occupied my full attention even while no pictures were being taken. Between canopy glare, turbulence, and twisting against a corset-like harness, I was happy some days to get any pictures at all. The extreme maneuvering and high G forces were always there, and I learned just to endure them throughout the process.

In photographing the diamond formation from within, I wanted to give the reader a more natural perspective, and therefore limited my use of super wide angle lenses. Due to the incredible tightness of the formation, however, some degree of wide angle was often necessary to make the picture.

The photographic challenges confronting me in the making of this book were numerous, and would make a whole separate story in themselves. Sometimes just getting in place to photograph the show was an adventure. At Traverse City, a wet and bouncing speedboat ride got me to a larger boat used for a show center point. In the exchange, there was that heartstopping moment of seeing my very full camera bag dangling precariously over deep Lake Michigan as it was handed from person to person on its way up to the deck, where its nervous owner was waiting. Cleveland saw a precarious climb to the very top of the control tower, while the end of the pier at Pensacola Beach, complete with fish hooks, bait, and disgruntled fishermen, was a new challenge in equipment management.

In the end, nearly 20,000 images were shot, with less than 200 selected for use in the book. Only two slide films were used, Kodak Lumiere and Kodachrome. Black and white print film was used during the performance briefing to capture the character portraits of the pilots; by mutual

182

BLUE ANGELS *A Portrait of Gold*

Call Sign:
PUNCHY

EPILOGUE

understanding, no flash was used so as not to interfere with their undivided concentration during this most critical time. Nikon cameras and lenses were used throughout, with some autofocus used on ground shots, while all aerial photos were focused manually. My Nikon F3 now has the distinction of having flown at Mach 3.4 and of having survived the Double Farvel.

The project, as a whole, was as great a challenge as I could ask for in one summer. Though much of it seemed like hard work at the time, I can recall the experience now only as a pleasure. Fighter pilots are not much different from each other, whether Navy or Air Force, and my past helped me to both better understand these men and enjoy being around them. The pointed humor that they directed my way was as welcome as the cups of ice water I gratefully downed immediately after flying, and no, I didn't wear my G-suit. Something about peer pressure.

Though they won't be found on the pages of this book, certain images will forever stay with me from my time with the Blue Angels: the happy faces of the critically ill children at St. Jude's Hospital; Lawman's grin near the end of the season when he said, "Only five more debriefings to go!"; that serious, wounded look on Snooze's face during a particularly bad debriefing; the crunching pitch-up to land; dinner at the Boss' home; the horror of watching a single film cartridge float in front of my visor during the zero G push into the Double Farvel; the desolate quiet of El Centro, where crumpled blue metal from years past still litters the desert in places; and one 4th of July in Traverse City, Michigan, when – while being escorted past the throngs of well-wishers lining the narrow streets and waving the American flag – an exhuberant motorcycle cop pulled his Harley up alongside our caravan and yelled over to us, "Is this a great country, or what?"

Meeting Dave Scheuer was one of the most enjoyable surprises of my year's journey. He and I were actually together once before, at my first air show in 1958. As the Grumman representative to the Blue Angels, though, he had no time then to talk with a little kid staring at his company's neatly parked blue jets. I am grateful that he had time 36 years later, in the comfort of his home, to share with me his recollections of the team's early days. Thanks, "Grandfather," for confirming everything I had always thought was special about the Tiger jet and that wonderful era of Blue Angel flying.

Special thanks to Butch Voris, Blue Angel #1, for taking part in the project and for being the only one who, finally, after much prying, would admit that the Blues were the best – and meaning it. I needed to hear that. Thanks, Butch, for starting something long ago that has impressed many of us over the years – some of us enough to want to write a book about it.

In the end, I realized that my experience in putting this book together closely paralleled the Blue Angel experience I sought to accurately portray.

After a year on the road, I felt exhausted from the travel, and had lugged my camera bags through enough hotels. I approached my aerial photography with extremely high and exacting expectations in much the same way as the pilots approached the precision of their flying. Similar to their debriefings, I too experienced many frustrations while critiquing my film. Like the team, I found more joy and satisfaction in the acceptance and trust of "the guys" than in any public acclaim or attention offered by others. Thanks, guys, for the four minutes of stick time. It is entered in gold in my log book.

When the team began anew in El Centro, winter training for me came in the form of concentrating in front of a computer for months, trying to build something out of a mountain of slides and the scribbled pages of a full diary. My remembrance of the team's perseverance and enthusiasm often helped me keep going during some difficult days.

I feel fortunate in having spent time with these very hard working people. They showed a pride in their work that is refreshing in today's world. They often made me laugh, and challenged me in many different ways. I miss being around them now. I understand better, too, why it was always so easy to say, "Glad to be here, Boss."

I sure was.

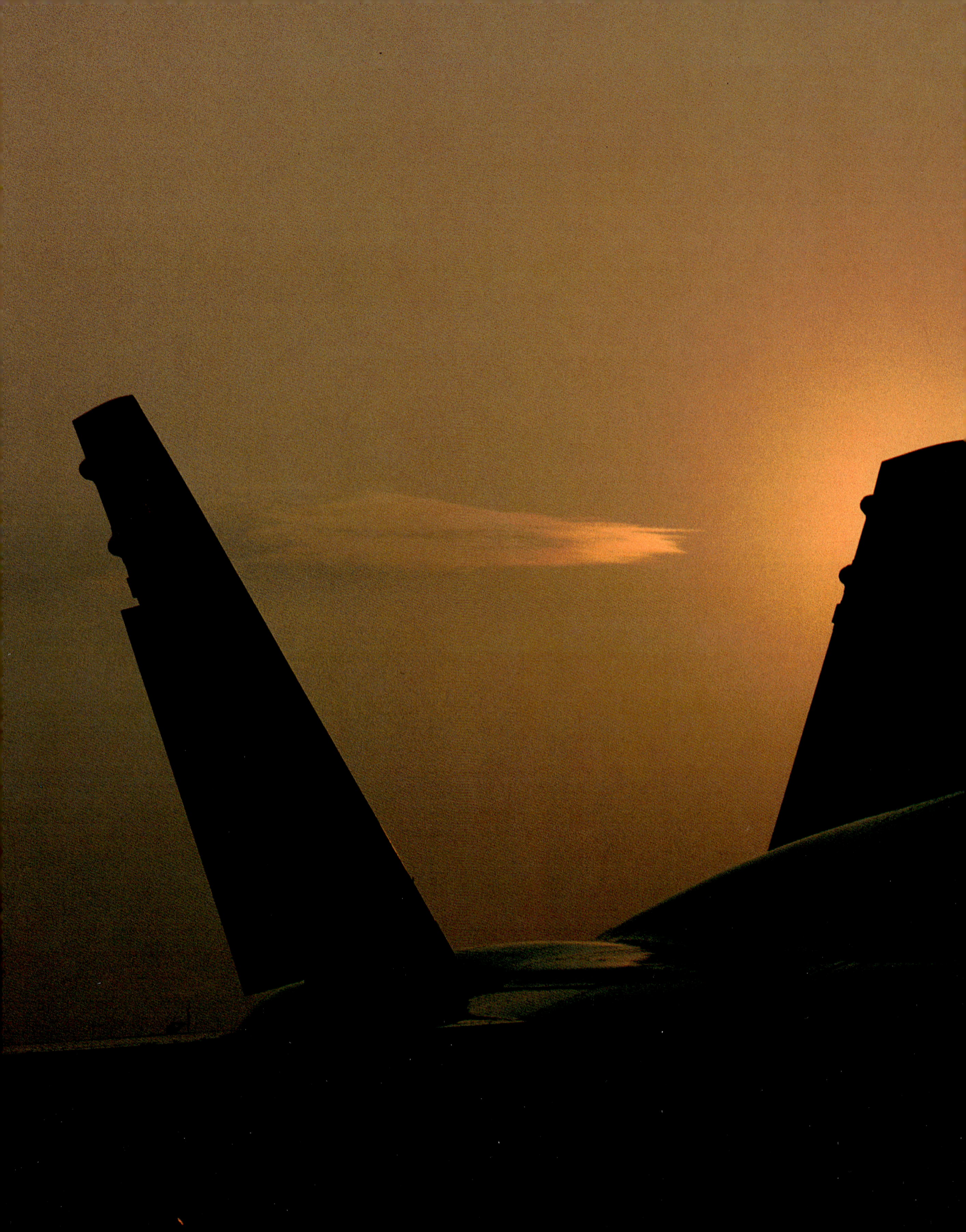

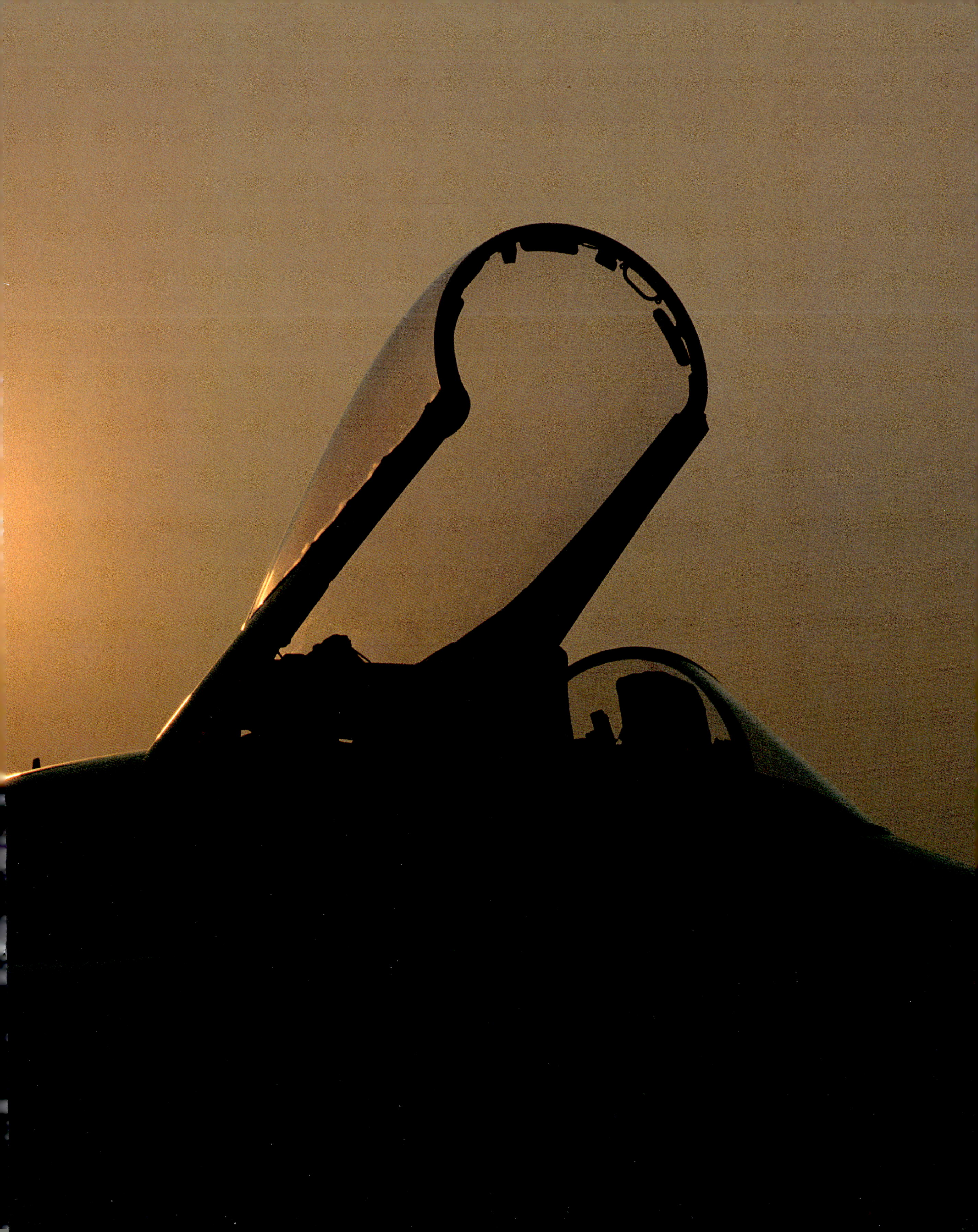

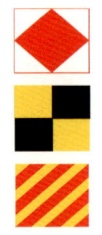

Roll Call

BLUE ANGELS PILOTS / PORTRAIT OF GOLD

BOSS
Cdr Bob Stumpf USN — #1 CO / Flight Leader

LAWMAN
Capt Ben Hancock USMC — #2 Right Wing

SNOOZE
LCdr Scott Anderson USN — #3 Left Wing

DINO
LCdr Doug Thompson USN — #4 Slot Pilot

HOOPS
LCdr Dave Stewart USN — #5 Lead Solo

TIMBER
Lt Rick Young USN — #6 Opposing Solo

BLUE ANGELS OFFICERS / PORTRAIT OF GOLD

Lt Dave Kidwell USN – DADDY		#7 Narrator
Lt Rob Surgeoner USN – SURGE		#8 Events Coordinator
Capt Joe Michalek USMC – HEYJOE		C-130 Pilot
Capt Craig Williams USMC – WILBUR		C-130 Pilot
Capt Pat DeLong USMC – BUBBA		C-130 Pilot
Lt Mark Evans USN – MO		Maintenance Officer
Lt Perry Bechtle MC USNR – DOC		Flight Surgeon
LCdr John Ottery USN – OTTER		Administrative Officer
Lt John Kirby USN – CUBBY		Public Affairs Officer
LCdr Rich Whelan USN – CORNDOG		Supply Officer

BLUE ANGELS CREW CHIEFS / PORTRAIT OF GOLD

AFCM James H Ellison	1994
ADC(AW) Michael Garrett	1994
GYSGT Dave Austin USMC	1994
GYSGT Robert L Benton USMC	1994
GYSGT Tom Blackburn USMC	1994
ATC(AW) Gregory J Block	1994
AKC(AW) Jean Gregg	1994
AZC(AW) Kathryn R Hall	1994
MSGT William W Pahl USMC	1994
AECS(AW) Paul Slavin	1994

Special thanks are due to the 1994 members of the United States Navy Flight Demonstration Squadron — the one and only Blue Angels.

BLUE ANGELS TEAM / PORTRAIT OF GOLD

AO2(AW) Willie J Adams	1994
AME2(AW) Pete Amendolare	1994
AK1 Jack Bartlett	1994
AK2 Roberto E Benitez	1994
AE2 Steve Bowman	1994
YN2 Frank B Campbell	1994
AMS2 Todd E Campbell	1994
AMS2(AW) Allen R Castillo	1994
PR3 Steven K Christie	1994
SGT Jess Chacon USMC	1994
CPL Charles M Clark USMC	1994
YN2 Terry L Coddington	1994
AD1 Angel Colon	1994
AME2 Darrin J Cook	1994
PH2 Jay G Cornelius	1994
AD1 Mary Correa	1994
AMS1(AW) Jerome G Czubinski	1994
AZ1(AW) Kenneth J Daniels	1994
AK2 Brad Dark	1994
SGT James E Driscoll USMC	1994
AZ1(AW) Donald L Easler	1994
AT2 Ike Edwards	1994
AMH2 John A Eggler	1994
AZ2 Derek A Enochs	1994
AK2 Julio Estrada	1994
AMS2 Scott A Evans	1994
AN Peter F Fabey	1994
AME2 Jacqueline E Fauria	1994
PR1 Mark C Filtranti	1994
SGT Ed Flanagan USMC	1994
AS2 Peter F Ford	1994
AMH2 Lewis Freeman	1994
AMH2(AW) Scott Freund	1994
AE1 Hoss Fugate	1994
AT1(AW) Richard W Gaines	1994
AE1 Gerald F Gantar	1994
AD2(AW) John Garland	1994
AME2 Gino J Grippo	1994
AT2 Todd Hall	1994
AT2(AW/SW) Ronnie C Harper	1994
YN1(AW) Frances E Heibult	1994
SGT Timothy S Hogan USMC	1994
AN James A Johns	1994
AS1 Michael P Kipp	1994
AMS2(AW) Richard K Kraemer	1994
AE2(AW) Kenneth L Kuchler	1994
PR1 Frederick F Lavasseur	1994
AD1(AW) Brian A Limer	1994
AMS2 Felix A Mata	1994
AD1 Todd E Melber	1994
SGT Paul M Melchior USMC	1994
HM1 William E Merritt	1994
AMH2 John D Milanek	1994
AD2(AW) Timothy A Miller	1994
AMH2 Cheryll D Miller	1994
AMH2 Steven Miller	1994
AK1(AW) Jimmy Montavon	1994
AT2 Jeffery Moss	1994
AE2 Thomas Nance	1994
DM2(AW) Nadine Nelson	1994
AME1 Antonio M Ocampo	1994
AN Cassondra L Osborn	1994
DM2 Christopher Ostrander	1994
JO1 Robert F J Pailthorpe	1994
AMS3 Kevin Parrish	1994
AN Stephanie D Percival	1994
YN2 Eddie Phillips	1994
AMS2 Gerald E Poncet	1994
AD1 Hugo Rodriguez	1994
AE1(AW) Jerry Rodriguez	1994
AMS3 Richard A Ruzbarsky	1994
AMS1(AW) Frank Ruzzene	1994
AMS2 Charles Scheck	1994
AMS2(AW) John D Sedam	1994
YN3 Wayne E Smith	1994
AT2 Tim Stopak	1994
AD2(AW) Foster L Stringer	1994
AK1(AW) Bonifacio Te	1994
AO1(AW) Allen J Thomas	1994
SSGT Leonard Tippett II USMC	1994
AN Lyndon Valbuena	1994
AMS2(AW) James R Wade	1994
AZ2(AW) John P Weir Jr	1994
AME2 Mark Wilhelm	1994
SSGT Thomas Winkelbauer USMC	1994
AE2 Keith Wright	1994
AE3 Gordon Zimmer	1994

FIFTY YEARS OF EXCELLENCE / FLIGHT ROSTER OF BLUE ANGELS PILOTS / 1946 TO 1996

Cdr Donnie Cochran	1986-1988 / 1995
Maj Ben Hancock USMC	1994-95
LCdr Dave Kidwell	1994-95
LCdr Scott Anderson	1993-95
LCdr Rick Young	1993-95
Lt Mark Provo	1995
Lt Ryan Scholl	1995
Lt Tom Munson	1995
Cdr Bob Stumpf	1993-1994
LCdr Doug Thompson	1992-1994
LCdr Dave Stewart	1992-1994
Lt Rob Surgeoner	1993-1994
Capt Greg Wooldridge	1991-1993
LCdr Larry Packer	1992-1993
Capt Ken Switzer USMC	1991-1993
LCdr Pat Rainey	1991-1992
LCdr John Foley	1990-1992
LCdr Randy Duhrkopf	1991-1992
LCdr Lee Grawn	1989-1991
LCdr Dave Inman	1990-1991
Lt Matt Seamon	1989-1991
Capt Pat Moneymaker	1989-1990
Maj Chase Moseley USMC	1990
LCdr Doug McClain	1988-1990
Lt Bruce Dillard	1989-1990
Capt Kevin Lauver USMC	1988-1989
LCdr Mark Ziegler	1988-1989
LCdr Cliff Skelton	1987-1989
Capt Gil Rud	1986-1988
LCdr Wayne Molnar	1986-1988
Lt Mike Campbell	1987-1988
LCdr David Anderson	1985-1987
Capt Mark Bircher USMC	1985-1987
LCdr Pat Walsh	1985-1987
LCdr Curt Watson	1983-1986
Maj Bill Campbell USMC	1985-1986
Cdr Larry Pearson	1984-1985
Lt Andy Caputi	1984-1985
LCdr Mike Gershon	1984-1985
Maj Mark Lauritzen USMC	1983-1984
LCdr Scott Anderson	1982-1984
LCdr Chris Ives	1983-1984
LCdr John Virden	1983-1984
Cdr Dave Carroll	1982-1983
LCdr Jim Ross	1979-1980 / 1982-1983
Maj Tim Dineen USMC	1981-1982
Lt Kevin Miller	1981-1982
LCdr Bob Stephens	1981-1982
LCdr Stu Powrie	1981
Lt Randy Clark	1980-1982
Lt Bud Hunsucker	1981-1982
Cdr Denny Wisely	1980-1981
LCdr Jim Horsley	1980-1981
LCdr Jack Ekl	1979-1981
Maj Fred Stankovich USMC	1979-1980
LCdr Mike Nord	1978-1980
Lt Kent Horne	1979-1980
Cdr Bill Newman	1978-1979
LCdr Bruce Davey	1977-1979
LCdr Jerry Tucker	1973-1974 / 1979
Capt Dan Keating USMC	1977-1978
LCdr Don Simmons	1977-1978
LCdr John Miller	1976-1978
Lt Mike Curtin	1978
Lt Ray Sandelli	1977-1978
Cdr Casey Jones	1976-1977
LCdr Vance Parker	1974-1975 / 1977
Lt Al Cisneros	1975-1977
Lt Jim Bauer	1975-1977
Lt Nile Kraft	1976
Capt Bill Holverstott USMC	1975-1976
Lt John Patton	1974-1976
Lt Denny Sapp	1975-1976
Cdr Tony Less	1974-1975
Lt John Chehansky	1973-1975
Capt Ken Wallace	1954-1955 / 1961-1963 / 1974
LCdr Marlin Wiita	1973-1974
Capt John Fogg USMC	1973-1974
Lt Chuck Newcomb	1972-1974
LCdr Skip Umstead	1970-1973
Lt Steve Lambert	1972-1973
Capt Mike Murphy USMC	1972-1973
LCdr Don Bently	1972-1973
Lt Bill Beardsley	1971-1972
Lt Bill Switzer	1971-1972
Lt Gary Smith	1972
Lt Larry Watters	1972
Lt Lou Lalli	1970-1972
Cdr Harley Hall	1970-1971
LCdr JD Davis	1970-1971
Capt Kevin O'Mara USMC	1970-1971
Lt Jim Maslowski	1970-1971
Lt Dick Schram	1969-71
Lt Steve Shoemaker	1969-1970
Lt Ernie Christensen	1969-1970
Cdr Bill Wheat	1967-1969
Lt Rick Adams	1968-1969
Lt Rick Millson	1968-1969
Lt John Allen	1967-1969
Capt Vince Donile USMC	1967-1969
Lt Smokey Tolbert	1968
Lt Bill Worley	1968
Lt Hal Loney	1967-1968
Lt Fred Wilson	1966-1968
Lt Norm Gandia	1966-1967
Lt Dave Rottgering	1966-1967
Lt Red Hubbard	1965-1967
Capt Fred Craig USMC	1965-1967
Capt Ron Thompson USMC	1967
Lt Frank Gallagher	1967
Cdr Bob Aumack	1964-1966
Lt Frank Mezzadri	1964-1966
LCdr Dick Oliver	1964-1966
Lt Mike Van Ort	1966
Lt Bob McDonough	1964-1965
LCdr Bob Cowles	1963-1965
Capt John Kretsinger USMC	1963-1964
Lt Dick Langford	1962-1964
Lt George Neale	1962-1964
Lt Dan Macintyre	1961-1963
Lt Lew Chatham	1961-1963
Lt Hank Giedzinski	1961-1962
Capt Doug MacCaughey USMC	1960-1962
Cdr Zeb Knott	1959-1961
Lt Bill Rennie	1960-1961
Lt Duke Ventigmiglia	1960-1961
Lt John Rademacher	1960
Lt Chuck Elliott	1960
Lt Bill Sherwood	1959
Lt Bob Rasmussen	1957-1959
Lt Herb Hunter	1957-1959
LCdr Jack Dewenter	1958-1959
Lt John Damian	1958-1959
Capt Stoney Mayock USMC	1958-1959
Lt Don McKee	1959
Lt Skip Campanella	1959
Lt Mark Perrault	1957-1959
Cdr Nick Glasgow	1958
1st Lt Tom Jefferson USMC	1957
Cdr Ed Holley	1957-1958
Lt Ed McKellar	1953-1956
Cdr Zeke Cormier	1954-1956
Lt Bruce Bagwell	1955-1957
Lt Nello Pierozzi	1955-1957
Lt Bill Gureck	1955-1956
Lt Lefty Schwartz	1956-1957
Capt Chuck Holloway USMC	1956
Capt Ed Rutty USMC	1955
LCdr Dick Newhafer	1949 / 1954-1955
Lt Dayl Crow	1953-1954
Lt Red Riedl	1955
Capt Pete Olson USMC	1955
Capt Chuck Hiett USMC	1954
LCdr Frank Graham	1949-1950 / 1952-1953
LCdr Ray Hawkins	1948-1950 /1952-1953
Lt Frank Jones	1952-1953
Lt Auz Aslund	1953-1954
Lt Buddy Rich	1952-1953
Lt Tom Jones	1952
Lt Pat Murphy	1952-1953
Lt Mac MacKnight	1948-1949 / 1952-1953
LCdr Whitey Feightner	1952
Lt Bud Wood	1952
Lt Jake Robcke	1948-1950
LCdr Johnny Magda	1949-1950
LCdr Dusty Rhodes	1947-1950
Lt(jg) Fritz Roth	1948-1950
Lt George Hoskins	1948-1950
Lt Ralph Hanks	1950
Lt Ed Oliphant	1949-1950
Lt Ed Mahood	1949
Lt Bob Longworth	1948-1949
Lt Hal Heagerty	1947-1949
Lt(jg) Billy May	1946-1948
LCdr Bob Clarke	1946-1948
Lt Bob Thelen	1947-1948
Lt Chuck Knight	1946-1947
Lt Al Taddeo	1946-1947
Lt Wick Wickendoll	1946-1947
Lt(jg) Gale Stouse	1946
Lt Mel Cassidy	1946
Lt(jg) Robby Robinson	1946
Lt JW Barnitz	1946-1947
Cdr Butch Voris	1946-1947 / 1952